MIC

CMC

The Italian undercover CIA and Mossad station
and the assassination of JFK

Copyright

What kind of peace do I mean? What kind of peace do we seek? Not a Pax Americana enforced on the world by American weapons of war. Not the peace of the grave or the security of the slave. I am talking about genuine peace, the kind of peace that makes life on earth worth living, the kind that enables men and nations to grow and to hope and to build a better life for their children – not merely peace for Americans but peace for all men and women– not merely peace in our time but peace for all time. [...]
So, let us not be blind to our differences –but let us also direct attention to our common interests and to the means by which those differences can be resolved. And if we cannot end now our differences, at least we can help make the world safe for diversity. For, in the final analysis, our most basic common link is that we all inhabit this small planet. We all breathe the same air. We all cherish our children's future. And we are all mortal.

John Kennedy

My father believed the Warren Report was a shoddy piece of craftsmanship. He publicly supported the Warren Commission report but privately he was dismissive of it. My father thought that somebody [else] was involved. The evidence at this point I think is very, very convincing that it was not a lone gunman.

Robert F. Kennedy Jr.

For Heather Heyer,
Telford Taylor,
August Landmesser,
Albino Luciani,
Pier Paolo Pasolini

Hi,

I wrote this book for the same reason you are reading it: because one late November day, I lost a loved one, killed by rifle crossfire, as you did.

Because one day in early August, I lost a daughter of only three years old, killed by a neo-fascist bomb in a railway station, as you did.

Because, on another day in August, I lost another daughter, mown down by a car driven by a racist, as you did.

Because, one day just before mid-December, I lost a brother in a bank; he too killed by a neo-fascist explosive device, as you did.

When every human being understands that the deaths in Dallas, Bologna, Charlottesville, Milan, were our loved ones, our relatives, then this will be a better world.

CMC
The Italian undercover CIA and Mossad station and the assassination of JFK

INTRODUCTION

A short 1959 film clip by LUCE, the Institute of Italian Cinema (Istituto Cinematografico Italiano LUCE), [1] recounts the inauguration of the *Centro Mondiale Commerciale* (World Trade Center) offices in the Roman district of Eur a year after its establishment in Italy, in a high-profile ceremony attended by the most powerful figures of the political elite in Italy at that time. The film shows, next to the name *Centro Mondiale Commerciale*, the logo Permindex, the head company founded by the Canadian Louis Bloomfield. It is the same *Centro Mondiale Commerciale* which employed Clay Shaw, an American businessman who, in 1967, as a result of collected evidence, became the chief suspect in the main judicial inquest into the death of John Fitzgerald Kennedy, overseen by Jim Garrison, then New Orleans District Attorney. Garrison was not fooled by the American government's version of events, provided by the Warren Commission, which concluded that the killing was a lone nut's action; reason why, as permitted by law, the DA reopened the case in a way so trustworthy that, once revived worldwide, thanks to the impact of the movie JFK by Oliver Stone, it was able to generate a movement of public opinion strong enough to persuade the US authorities to issue the so-called Assassinations Disclosure Act, which generated the Assassination Records Review Board. This organization put together new evidence and finally unveiled other undisclosed evidence, revealing the full validity of the New Orleans inquest with the outcome that John Kennedy was killed in a plot against him.

The ground-breaking news is that I own what no one else has ever been able to acquire: the company papers of *Centro Mondiale Commerciale*. Thanks to these papers, I can now show you each and all of the other extremely important names alongside that of Clay Shaw in

---

[1] https://youtu.be/BlPXfrbBRAc?t=96

the company. And they are not only names that have never ever emerged till now, but they will also give you the clearest and most innovative picture of the death of John Kennedy ever made: a conspiracy fueled by an international masonic pact against JFK, and involving the CIA, Mossad, and Italian Intelligence. [2]

What you are about to read is exclusive and brand new. No other book can disclose what this one can about the assassination of JFK. Let us begin.

---

[2] You will find a selection of the CMC papers used for this book in the Appendix. Besides, I also created a specific account on Flickr: www.flickr.com/photos/mettacmc. There, you can examine these same papers in a large variety of sizes. For your further convenience, they are all also arranged in an album: https://flic.kr/s/aHsmk94WZo. This is its short URL: https://bit.ly/2RQD7PV.

THE MASONIC PACT AGAINST JFK

On July 7, 1960 an alliance agreement was signed in Rome between US Freemasons and *Grande Oriente* (Grand Orient), the most high-profile masonic community of Freemasons in Italy. At the signing ceremony, two people on behalf of Italy were present: Antonio Trabucchi, a representative of the government of the peninsula, and Publio Cortini, the Grand Master of the Italian freemasonry. For the United States, there were, instead, the Ambassador James Zellerbach and a certain Frank Gigliotti. Apparently, the event had no mysterious connotations. However, years later it became clear that this ceremony, which seemed to be all above board, had secret clauses, the first of which was, as I said, to stop Kennedy. Let us see how this was discovered.

In 1981, a serious danger became apparent in Italy: the creation, from the beginning of the 1960s, of an occult super lodge of Freemasons called P2. Its chief was a fascist named Licio Gelli. This P2 lodge had schemed and continued to scheme anti-democratically, protected by the complicit extreme right and both the Italian and American Intelligence. And in fact, it is possible to verify how in the subversive P2 there were at least 43 generals and 8 admirals, all the heads of Italian intelligence, as well as 44 members of the Italian House of Deputies and Senate, most of them belonging to the *Democrazia Cristiana* party, the major political party in the country at that time. Moreover, P2 even included important members of the fascist military dictatorship which had come to power in Argentina in 1976.

Prompted by strong public indignation, the Italian authorities were forced to conduct a parliamentary commission of enquiry, led by Tina Anselmi. Following enquiries, the commission seized many masonic documents. My point is that one of these was a letter which spoke about Kennedy. It was sent from the Grand master of the Freemasons Enzo Milone to the Christian Democratic parliamentarian Elio Rosati. Dated September 24, 1960, it was therefore written just two months before the US Presidential elections which saw JFK stand against the Republican Richard Nixon. Milone writes:

I attach a series of documents which can provide full information about everything that some leaders of American Masonry did to make waves in masonic organizations in various European countries about a certain political task.

Effectively, Milone enclosed a full copy of an article published by a US masonic magazine which laid down the strong invitation to vote against JFK in the forthcoming November elections. Milone's letter continues:

Since Kennedy began talking about his candidacy, articles and letters began to come out of the US crying foul. America, a country built with the contribution of Masonry, where every President before becoming one must become a Freemason, could actually have a Catholic President! An American President cannot follow two leaders! America and the Pope […]
Thus, the collaboration asked of European Freemasons: propagate as much as possible the protestant idea - influence Italian immigrants in the USA to vote against Kennedy […]
For this purpose, to Italy came Doctor Frank Gigliotti, protestant pastor and a representative of American Masonry.

If it weren't for the tragic end he would meet in Dallas, this alleged need to stop JFK because he was a Catholic might be really laughable. We will in fact have many opportunities to see how close all the circles of right-wing world politics were at that time to the Church of Rome. The sincere point in the letter arrives when it states that the powers that be hated Kennedy and considered him a menace for his not being part of the Freemasonry.

But at the same time the Italian commission of inquest was investigating, it emerged that Gigliotti was also a CIA agent. What I add now is that he was a CIA agent with great power, as demonstrated in another letter, this time written by Gigliotti himself on

10

30 September 1952 to the then President of the USA in person: Truman. [3] In this letter Gigliotti showed a decisive tone of command by asking Truman to fire Bedell Smith, who was then director of the CIA. Gigliotti justified this request by accusing Smith of being too soft on Communism. Here it is:

My dear President Truman: Some months ago while talking with Margaret Vaughn at their home I told her that I felt that General Bedell Smith would let you down the first opportunity that he had […].
[…]
I want you to know, my dear President, that we have loved you and respected you and defended your flank in season and out of season, through the churches, through political organisations, and before the general public for after all, I feel that no President of the United States has given of himself more wholeheartedly that have in solving the problems that have confronted us as a sovereign people. The statement of General Bedell Smith last night that 'There is no security organisation in the government of the United States into which communists have not infiltrated themselves' is a shame upon him for you gave him every authority and every opportunity to clean them out. What has he been doing all this time besides nursing his ulcers if this is true, and to a certain degree it is true? The only exception may be the F.B.I.
You will remember that a little over a year ago I made the statement that what we needed to head Central Intelligence was a man who gave ulcers to the enemy and not one who allowed the enemy to produce ulcers in his own system and in the thinking of the Nation. [...]
[…] I think, along with many others of your friends, that the Intelligence of the United States as centralised in Bedell Smith is at the lowest ebb it has ever been in the history of the United States.
General Bedell Smith has made Central Intelligence Agency a boarding house for retired admirals and generals at a rate of $50 a day or more, plus their retired pay that they are already receiving to the extent that the consultant staff of C.I.A. is often referred to as Smith's boarding house for broken-down flag officers […].
I am sending you this information as your friend, and I am asking these questions not only as your friend, but as one who has consecrated and dedicated his

---

[3] Letter, Gigliotti to Truman, September 30, 1952. Papers of Harry S. Truman, Harry S. Truman Library, White House Central Files, Confidential Files. - Courtesy of Gale. Gale Document Number: GALE|CK2349239176

life to helping make our beloved America a place where future generations will be proud of the fact that you were President of the United States and that those who lived before them did, under God, the things that they felt were right so that free institutions might be preserved.

Mr. Smith should be brought to task. Again I say, if these things were true, why didn't he tell them to you before instead of giving them to the newspapers just before elections. I feel that he has betrayed all of the confidence that you have placed in him.

With regards and prayers, I remain
Your friend,
Frank B. Gigliotti.

As a matter of fact, Bedell Smith was actually fired; and it was exactly thank to this firing that, from February 1953, Allen Dulles reached the top of the CIA. The latter was a Freemason himself and, as we shall see, always treated Kennedy as an enemy. This letter to Truman is also needed to understand a subsequent letter, this time directly relevant to JFK, and written on 6 August 1960: exactly while Gigliotti was making the anti-Kennedy pact with the Italian Masonry. [4] It was addressed from Gigliotti to Nixon, promising the solemn commitment of the Freemasons to leave no stone unturned in helping him to victory against JFK. This letter becomes more disturbing when you know that the aforementioned *Commissione Anselmi* (Anselmi Commission) had determined that another secret clause of Gigliotti's pact between the Italian and American Masonry was that of raising masonic lodges in Italy commanded by the CIA and NATO.

But in order to complete the argument, we should move on to January 24, 2011, when a member of the P2 lodge, named Bruno Rozera, allowed himself to be interviewed for the well-known Italian weekly magazine *L'Espresso*. [5] In his interview, Rozera revealed

---

[4] Letter, Gigliotti to Nixon, August 6, 1960. Richard M. Nixon Pre-Presidential Papers, Richard M. Nixon, Presidential Library, Yorba Linda, CA, Vice President General Correspondence, Series 320, Box 567
[5] L'ESPRESSO: Fabrizio Gatti, *Cent'anni di trame*, January 21, 2011

that the organizer of Gigliotti's mission in Italy culminating in the pact against Kennedy, was Giuseppe Pièche. A former general under Mussolini, Pièche was surrounded by protectors and acquaintances so important as to enable him to not only save himself from the consequences of being a central figure under the dictatorship, but even allowing him to become an equally eminent figure, once again, of the *Guerra non ortodossa* (Non-orthodox war) against communism under the auspices of NATO and the CIA. In fact, Giuseppe Pièche, with the complicity of the then Italian Interior Minister Mario Scelba, created and directed a *Servizio Antincendi* (Fire Service) which in reality obscured a *Stay-Behind* structure. He was helped in this venture by a soon-to-be member of *P2*, Edgardo Sogno, who, in the 1990s, made several public declarations clearly qualifying this *Antincendi* as a *NATO* project linked to the Gladio network. [6] In effect, over the years evidence emerged that show how Pièche, through the *Antincendi*, had abusively filled secret files on notable individuals in the Italian progressive movements – unions, show business, politics – and that he had also allowed and protected neo-fascist groups such as the *Armata Italiana della Libertà* (Italian Freedom Army), the *Fronte Antibolscevico Italiano* (Italian Anti-Bolshievic Front), and of the far-right party *Movimento Sociale* (Social Movement). [7] Confirmation of this can be found in CIA documents now declassified. In one, dated 1948, we can read, for example: [8]

---

[6] LA STAMPA: Gianni Bisio, *Sogno smentisce l'ex ministro: non ricorda*, November 1, 1990; Ivano Barbiero, Cosimo Mancini, *Sogno: il governo mi finanziava*, November 5, 1990. See also the ITALIAN DOCUMENT: Commissione Stragi, Doc. XXIII n. 64 VOLUME III, Resoconti stenografici delle riunioni dell'Ufficio di Presidenza e degli incontri seminariali

[7] AVANTI!: *I "pieni poteri" a Scelba aprirebbero la via alla dittatura*, May 12, 1951; See also De Lutiis, *Storia dei servizi segreti in Italia*; Cipriani, *Sovranità limitata*; Murgia, *Ritorneremo!*

[8] General CIA Records, CIA-RDP82-00457R001400800002-0, *Communist insurrection not expected by the Italian Government*, April 15, 1948

General Giuseppe Pieche was appointed in March by Minister Scelba to serve as his personal aide (with the rank of prefect) for the coordination of activity relating to public order in the event of an insurrection [of Marxists]

And in another: [9]

Gen. PIECHE, recently appointed head of a new special office under the Ministry of Interior [Scelba], to act as his personal secretary.

If those are not enough, some Italian Intelligence documents reveal a strong symbiosis between the *Anticendi* and the so-called Gehlen Organization; [10] that is, the West German spy network created, with the will of the CIA, from the ashes of the *Fremde Heere Ost*, formerly spies of the *Oberkommando des Heeres*, Supreme Command of the Nazi Army. And in fact, both the *FHO* and the Gehlen Organization, later renamed *Bundesnachrichtendienst*, were commanded by the Nazi Reinhard Gehlen, who remained head of the *Bundesnachrichtendienst* (more simply known as *BND*) until 1968. What is more, a right-wing formation called *Pace e Libertà* (Peace and Freedom) was created, co-run by Pièche and Sogno. [11] Well, the financer of *Pace e Libertà* was Allen Dulles, personally declared as such by Sogno himself, who so remembers: [12]

---

[9] CIA Special Collection, Nazi War Crimes Disclosure Act, Document Number (FOIA)/ESDN (CREST): 51966eca993294098d50a984, *Benuzzi Valerio 003*
[10] ITALIAN DOCUMENT: Procura della Repubblica di Brescia, Procedimento Penale Nr. 91/97 R.G.N.R. della c.d. "Strage di Piazza della Loggia". Annotazione a cura dell'Ispettore della Polizia di Stato Michele Cacioppo del Servizio Antiterrorismo della Direzione Centrale della Polizia di Prevenzione concernente l'esame della documentazione relativa all'organizzazione Gehlen" acquisita al SISMI
[11] ITALIAN DOCUMENT: *XII Legislatura. Commissione stragi. Il terrorismo, le stragi ed il contesto storico-politico. Proposta di relazione redatta dal Presidente della Commissione, senatore Giovanni Pellegrino*; see also Gianni Flamini, *I pretoriani di Pace e Libertà*
[12] Gianni Flamini, *I pretoriani di Pace e Libertà*; Claudio Gatti, *Rimanga tra noi*

I decided to go to America to ask my old friend Allen Dulles for help. Thanks to our ambassador in Washington I obtained an appointment with the head of the CIA and I explained to him in detail what our activities and needs were [...] He did not commit. He only said he would think about it. Time later, I got a telephone call from Alfredo Pizzoni, president of Credito Italiano [Italian Credit Bank] in Milan. We had been in the Resistance together. He called me into his office and said: "Eddy, I have to give you an envelope." I took it, opened it and found Dulles's first financial contribution. After that, Pizzoni continued to play the role of mediator, delivering amounts of money of between 5 and 15 million lire.

This declaration does deserve special attention also because the aforementioned Pizzoni was the companion of Corrado Bonfantini. This latter was, first of all, a CMC member, but also a person linked to both Sogno and P2 Freemason Michele Sindona. But a full description of Bonfantini will be given in another section of this book. Now it is really more opportune to return immediately to the confession of Rozera about Pièche, completing it with the first of many extraordinary revelations contained in the company papers which I finally found: that is, Giuseppe Pièche was also a member of the CMC Board of Directors. Not only that, but that Trabucchi who was previously mentioned as being present at the drawing-up of the pact between CIA and the Freemasons, was also a minister in the government headed by Fernando Tambroni. Tambroni was so right-wing that the aim of that Cabinet was to try and return Italy to fascist dictatorship. [13] The news is that Tambroni's son-in-law, Franco Micucci Cecchi was another member of *Centro Mondiale Commerciale*, company papers reveal. Therefore, there is ample evidence so far to sustain that CMC was behind the pact against JFK. And yet, there are still many other elements left. Let us explore them.

---

[13] See, for example, Adele Cambria, *Nove dimissioni e mezzo: le guerre quotidiane di una giornalista ribelle*; Pietro Di Loreto, *La difficile transizione*; IL SOLE 24 ORE: Andrea Romano, *La polizia segreta di Tambroni*, June 26, 2011; LOTTA CONTINUA: *Finché la banca va – Storia del Banco di Sicilia (1)*, August 2, 1972

THE *SACRO COLLEGIO DEL RITO* (SACRED PANEL OF RITES) OF 1981

Moving along to December 5, 1981:[14] the storm of the P2 scandal was at its height, so much so that Ms. Anselmi was already head of the once again cited commission that was investigating it. It was on this date that a meeting took place which needs recounting: it was the *Sacro collegio del rito* (Sacred Panel of Rites), the high assembly of top Italian Freemasons. Why was this meeting so important? Because a document was mentioned numerous times in the minutes of the meeting. This document, it was insisted, was highly classified – to the point, say the minutes, that the consequences of it becoming public were unthinkable. The Sovereign (a term in masonic jargon meaning he who chairs the meeting) added this plea:[15]

it must be kept strictly classified among [the other] Brothers as any mention of this matter could have negative effects on the Brothers and may even lead to panic, especially in certain sectors.

Who was in possession of the document? It was, according to the minutes, in the hands of Enzo Milone, who was also, as I explained before, the writer of the letter on September 24, 1960 to the Member of Parliament Elio Rosati in which he talks of the secret pact against Kennedy. Following great insistence by the select group of Freemasons, Enzo Milone himself summarized its contents. Which was this:

A member from the U.S.A. – Br[other] Frank GIGLIOTTI, member of the C.I.A. – arrived in Italy, contacted [the masonic group of] Piazza del Gesù [Jesus Square] and proposed a series of political and religious obligations for the unification of

---

[14] ITALIAN DOCUMENT: *Commissione P2. Allegati alla relazione. Doc. XXIII, n°2-quarter, Vol. III, Tomo I*
[15] ITALIAN DOCUMENT: *Commissione P2. Allegati alla relazione. Doc. XXIII, n°2-quarter, Vol. III, Tomo I*

Italian Freemasons (for example, an anti-clerical stance, oppose the nomination of Kennedy for President of the U.S.A., considering that, as a Catholic, he would not be able to serve two bosses: Church and State, etcetera.).

While this discussion was going on, GIGLIOTTI contacted the Grande Oriente (GAMBERINI) and [...] assured America that the unification of the two [masonic] families had already been accomplished. Consequently, America recognized Grande Oriente as the only legitimate Freemasonry in Italy.

At the same time, GIGLIOTTI managed to obtain privileges from the Italian government for Grande Oriente (lease of the headquarters of Palazzo Giustiniani for another 23 years for 83,100 Lire a month) as well as the recognition of Grande Oriente as the only existing Freemasonry in Italy.

These are exactly the same arguments that Milone spoke about in his letter to Rosati, but with *many* more clarifications and revelations. As I emphasized, we are first of all actually inside a meeting of *élite* Freemasons. Yet, despite this, the onlookers had to insist on being told what it was all about. This means that the pact against Kennedy was something so secretive and shocking that it was only known to a very reserved group of members and therefore, obviously, *extremely powerful* in the masonic world. Furthermore, here was Milone himself openly recognizing that Gigliotti was part of the CIA. Actually, more precisely, Milone read Gigliotti's actions as the result of Gigliotti being a member of the biggest spy agency of the United States. This fact is even clearer in the minutes of another later meeting, on January 23, 1982, of the *Sacro Collegio del Rito*. This is what was reported: [16]

GIGLIOTTI, with the power he had, especially as an agent of the CIA, managed [...] to obtain official recognition of the masonic headquarters in that Palazzo [Giustiniani] as the only, official, legal one.

Furthermore, here are members of the same Italian Masonry admitting that the privileges brought about by Gigliotti for his own

---

[16] ITALIAN DOCUMENT: *Commissione P2. Allegati alla relazione. Doc. XXIII, n°2-quarter, Vol. III, Tomo I*

institution were a bargaining chip. In fact, these privileges were given on condition that there must be an end to any internal resistance to the most daring and compromising of plans: stopping JFK. These plans, as we have seen, involved individuals in the CMC, like Pièche, or linked to the CMC, like Tambroni.

It should be noted, however, how Milone – in the meeting of December 5, 1981 – *concludes* his argument, which he himself started in 1960: [17]

Everything happening [today] has its matrix in what occurred in 1962.

Note the year. Milone does not say 1960, the date – I repeat – in which the pact to try and prevent Kennedy *becoming* President, using propaganda favoring the candidate Nixon, was struck. *No.* Milone says 1962; when Kennedy is *already* in the White House, and to stop him means something else; it means things like Dallas. 1962 – specifically – is above all the year in which Licio Gelli entered the Freemasonry. And also: 1962 is the year a secret deal was struck between the CIA and Giovanni De Lorenzo, a powerful member of Freemasonry and of Italian Intelligence. As we will see in the following pages, this clandestine pact was an important weapon in the struggle between right-wing American powers and JFK.

What is more, Milone also states: [18]

At this point the D.C. is afraid these documents could come out.

Let's examine that. If the DC (Christian Democratic Party) is worried, it means only one thing: those documents concern the involvement of DC leaders who at that time had governed Italy without interruption for decades thanks to the help of the CIA. The

---

[17] ITALIAN DOCUMENT: *Commissione P2. Allegati alla relazione. Doc. XXIII, n°2-quarter, Vol. III, Tomo I*

[18] ITALIAN DOCUMENT: *Commissione P2. Allegati alla relazione. Doc. XXIII, n°2-quarter, Vol. III, Tomo I*

CIA's help was also a bargaining tool as we will see further on. In fact, the DC obtained help with the obvious guarantee of making the country subservient to the will of the Central Intelligence Agency. But no less interesting is what, in that same December 5 meeting, was said by Franco Nataloni, a 33rd degree Freemason: [19]

if these papers were to get into the hands of the D.C. Tina ANSELMI, this could put all of us in trouble.

In short: not only were those papers about the involvement of highly-placed DC parliamentarians but, if the question were to get into the hands of an *honest* DC parliamentarian determined to get to the bottom of things such as Anselmi was, this could risk causing very serious trouble indeed. This possibility was becoming more concrete every day since this commission had already achieved the absolute contiguity between Gigliotti and Gelli, which it emphasized in the phrase: [20]

It emerges, moreover, **to our attention that Gelli appears on the scene when Giogliotti disappears,** according to a succession of times and interchange of people that is very striking

Certainly, a series of personal notes drafted by Anselmi, which today are publicly revealed, make explicit reference to the desire of top leaders of the Christian Democrats to close down the commission at all costs. [21] But how did Gelli come to have so much power? In answering this question, we can also clarify further the meaning of the phrase above about Gigliotti, and also dig deeper into the plot that led to the death of John Kennedy.

---

[19] ITALIAN DOCUMENT: *Commissione P2. Allegati alla relazione. Doc. XXIII, n°2-quarter, Vol. III, Tomo I*
[20] ITALIAN DOCUMENT: *Commissione parlamentare d'inchiesta sulla Loggia massonica P2*; Relazione di Maggioranza della Onorevole Tina Anselmi
[21] Anna Vinci, *La P2 nei diari segreti di Tina Anselmi*

JAMES J. ANGLETON'S *ITALIAN RESERVOIR*

I received a vital revelation concerning this point from Sergio Flamigni. As he had been a member of the aforementioned *Commissione Anselmi* and had spent many years studying the matter, he is widely known as one of the top experts on Licio Gelli. I managed, through Flamigni, [22] to learn about a crucial secret event in the final phases of WWII: the recruitment of Licio Gelli by James Angleton, the head at that time of the Italian Section of OSS, the precursor to the CIA. CIA which Angleton also became a member of, and with an even more important role, by the way. Flamigni's source was Peter Tompkins, who had previously been a top agent in the OSS in Italy exactly during WWII. Tompkins' source was in turn another top agent in the same organization: Max Corvo. This is notable because Corvo was a key figure in Operation Husky, the codename for the Allied landings in Sicily in 1943. The problem was that in order to guarantee the operation's success, Corvo paid a high price: alliance with the Mafia. And how was this done? Through a team of Corvo's trusted men, which included Gigliotti. This is clearly visible in a report of July 7, 1947 by Walter C. Dowling, then part of the US State Department, Division of South European Affairs, which says: [23]

I fear that Gigliotti, also a member of OSS, is trying to activate the old OSS gang in Italy as a way of fighting communism. It is well-known that the activities of that group, set up mainly by Italian Americans like Scamporini and Corvo, have always been of dubious value and most of them were sent home when Bob Joyce took the lead in Italy.

If that were not enough, it was this OSS gang that granted another significant recruitment: that of Michele Sindona. [24] Since this latter

---

[22] Series of emails and conversations during October 2017, through his collaborator Giulia Corradi
[23] Luigi Cipriani, *Appunti sull'anticomunismo dal dopoguerra ad oggi*
[24] Peter Tompkins, *Strategy of Terror*

later became a key figure inside P2, no doubt there exists a very strong tie between Angleton and P2. In fact, from that moment on, Angleton was the secret head of both Gelli and Sindona. This information is vital to the following series of events that I will narrate, which will take us straight to the heart of the plot against JFK.

CENTRO MONDIALE COMMERCIALE AND P2

In fact, we are now about to discover in how many infinite ways the CMC is indistinguishable from the masonic lodge P2 at the center of what must be the most disgraceful conspiracies endured by Italy. Conspiracies that are rooted in a deplorable piece of Italian history given the bloody title of *Strategia della Tensione* (Strategy of Tension). It means, to be clear, a series of attacks under the hidden cover of the CIA and NATO: acts of violence including bombs on trains and in public places; bloodbaths to frighten the populace into welcoming authoritarian governments. In fact, Gelli was found guilty of one of the worst episodes of violence, the *Strage di Bologna* (Bologna Massacre), when an explosive device set off by fascists in 1980 killed 85 people and injured over 200 more in the railway station of one of the most important cities in northern Italy. Well, among the papers of the CMC which I finally obtained, there are those pertaining to the IAHC. This is unsurprising because, as I will explain later in more detail, this IAHC was a CMC subsidiary. Instead, the surprise is that these IAHC papers reveal meetings of its Board of Directors in a very central place in Rome; that is, Piazza di Spagna (Spanish Square – near the Spanish Steps) at 72/A; or, as the report itself shows, "in the office of the lawyer Roberto Ascarelli."

To understand why this is a surprise, and why this is related to the lack of distinction between CMC and P2, we need to fully understand who Ascarelli was. The best way to do it is by looking at *Trame atlantiche* (Atlantic Plots), work of the aforementioned Flamigni. This book narrates the important early days of P2, showing how

Ascarelli was instrumental in Gelli's rise to the top of the lodge in the 1960s, despite the fact that Gelli was a Mussolini fanatic. Ascarelli strongly recommended Gelli to Giordano Gamberini, who was not only at the head of the masonic lodge *Grande Oriente* from 1961 to 1970, but as the investigations by the *Commissione Anselmi* discovered, he was also the trustee of the CIA inside the very same *Grande Oriente*. Flamigni perfectly encapsulates Gelli's rise in the following:

Gelli's past as a fascist and a member of the Italian fascist Republic of Salò which impeded his affiliation [until that moment], has actually become a guarantee of the anti-communist purpose which he will be required to fulfil.

The close link between Ascarelli and the fortunes of Gelli is also reaffirmed in the works of the *Commissione parlamentare d'inchiesta sulla P2* (Parliamentary commission of inquest on P2) chaired by Anselmi. She writes that "the Assistant Grand Master, Roberto Ascarelli, pointed out Licio Gelli to the Grand Master, Giordano Gamberini, recommending him as someone able to do great things for the [masonic] institution, in terms of converting qualified people." But the commission adds one more important element regarding Ascarelli: he was head of a lodge, the Hod, which, prior to joining P2, Gelli had been a part of. The commission also reveals that both Hod and P2 had their headquarters in exactly the same office belonging to Roberto Ascarelli, writing:

[Gelli] began reuniting the brothers already in P2 and those who would be joining, in the office of the lawyer Ascarelli in piazza di Spagna. Up to then the brothers of another very reserved lodge had met there. The Hod Lodge was considered by some as an antechamber and by others as a twin of P2. With Gelli's arrival, these brothers began to distinguish themselves with the label "*Ragruppamento Gelli-P2* [Gelli-P2 Group]".

Putting it all together, we discover a new and disturbing fact about CMC. The meeting place of its operations not only coincides with the meeting place of the *Raggruppamento Gelli-P2*, but it was also the same meeting point of the Hod Lodge, which sworn witnesses had defined as a precursor if not even a twin of P2. In other words, it means that the Hod Lodge headed by Roberto Ascarelli had the same relationship to P2 as the IAHC had to the CMC.

It should be noted that P2's beginnings in Piazza di Spagna 72/A was in later years confirmed by Gelli himself in the book interview *Parola di Venerabile* (The Venerable Word). When asked where the initiation of his new members took place, Gelli replied:

In the first phase we celebrated the initiation rituals [to P2] in Ascarelli's office, at number 72 in Piazza di Spagna, on the third floor. We were assisted by Virgilio Gaito, who at the time was an associate lawyer who would go on to become Grand Master of Goi. The ceremony lasted about an hour and a quarter because many ritual passages were skipped. Ascarelli initiated the new brothers and I was the witness. As it wasn't a masonic headquarters, we used a portable temple which we carried in a briefcase that we opened on the table. It had everything inside: a to-scale reproduction of the columns, the checkerboard floor, an altar that faced the east. The sword was foldable. For each initiation I provided Ascarelli with the new Freemason's curriculum vitae, so that, when the ceremony was finished, he could talk to the neophyte about his job and his experiences. In general, these conversations always ended up being about great historical figures.

When Licio Gelli stated that Piazza di Spagna 72/A was not a masonic headquarters, what he intended – please, pay attention – is that it was not a *manifest* headquarters, but a secret one. The typical architecture of a manifest masonic headquarters could not in fact be used because of this secrecy. That was the reason why the checkerboard floor, columns and altar were provided in miniature in the briefcase. The fact that it *was* a masonic secret headquarter is after all also demonstrated by what I just said before: Piazza di Spagna 72/A was no less the HQ of the Hod Lodge.

But there's more. Thanks to the CMC papers which I obtained, there is another surprise: the huge, unprecedented novelty of seeing Ascarelli and Virgilio Gaito appear in the CMC Board of Directors. Gaito, above all, is the one who, from December 18, 1993 to March 21, 1999, was destined to wear Gamberini's robe as the Grand Master of the *Grande Oriente d'Italia*. Besides, in 1962 the plot against JFK started involving a key figure of the Italian Intelligence and Freemasonry: Giovanni De Lorenzo, an individual who was closely linked to the CMC, as we will see. But to recount this event, we must begin with another *Centro Mondiale Commerciale* member: Carlo d'Amelio.

CAPOCOTTA'S BUILDING SPECULATION

When Carlo d'Amelio entered the *CMC*, he was already widely famous as an *élite* lawyer; in fact, he was the administrator of the assets of Casa Savoia. [25] Savoias were the Italian royal family when Italy was still a monarchy. This explained d'Amelio's jobs as economic advisor of *Immobiliare Marina Reale* (Marina Reale Real Estate) and vice-president of the Board of Directors of *Compagnia Sviluppo Marina Reale* (Marina Reale Development Company); [26] these were the administration companies of Capocotta, a well-known property estate, in that juncture, belonging to the Savoia family. [27] On this estate, the CMC attempted a massive building speculation which brings us to the Freemason General De Lorenzo.

The first news of the speculation broke out on March 5, 1967 in the Italian newspaper *Paese Sera* in an article by Mario Ugazzi. This newspaper no longer exists but at that time it had a wide readership, and great prestige. The headline was as eloquent as the article: *I Savoia venderanno Capocotta al gruppo del Centro Mondiale Commerciale*. (The Savoias to sell Capocotta to Centro Mondiale Commerciale group). This piece actually forms part of a large investigation

---

[25] *Who's who in Italy*, 1957 – 1958
[26] Documents in my possession
[27] PAESE SERA: *I personaggi del CMC-IAHC*, March 5, 1967; *Il chi è della finanza italiana*, 1962. On the strong links between d'Amelio and *Casa Savoia*, see, for example, CORRIERE DELLA SERA, *Vinta dai Savoia la causa contro lo Stato italiano*, February 27, 1963

which had occupied *Paese Sera*'s headlines for a number of issues. Even if these articles, missing in the company documents I instead own, do not offer the wealth of names and information which this book will exclusively be able to provide, the results of the newspaper's investigation are nevertheless worth noting, starting with its explanation of how the speculation began. Ugazzi described, in fact, that there had been problems at the start, but these had been completely resolved by the CMC thanks to the use of a well-known strategy in such cases: by changing the name of the company involved. So, the speculation reappeared under the aforementioned IAHC, the CMC subsidiary satellite, concocted by the *Centro Mondiale Commerciale* to muddy the waters and to carry out the plan *at any cost*. Ugazzi explicates:

[Giorgio] Mantello was still the managing director. The IAHC obtained the capital through Centro Mondiale Commerciale and the stockholders were always the same. In fact, the money arrived from Credito Internazionale di Ginevra [the Italian name for *Banque de Crédit International* in Geneva, also known as International Credit Bank], from De Famaco Anstaldt Vaduz, Miami Anstaldt Vaduz and from the Seligman bank in Basel, all through the Banca Nazionale del Lavoro [National Employment Bank].

This is strikingly similar to the situation, to give a practical example, of the *Sociedad Española de Automóviles de Turismo* (SEAT), which from 1950 to 1985 was the Spanish branch of the FIAT brand, and produced identical FIAT cars in Spain, except for the SEAT logo. After all, as I explained at the start, the same CMC was nothing other than the Italian branch of Permindex. In light of all this, it is certainly correct to state that the members of IAHC all belonged to CMC. As final proof that the two organizations were really the same thing, the reaffirmation lies in what the telephone operators answered to whoever, at that time, called the IAHC number: «*Centro Mondiale Commerciale*».

Anstalt – not *Anstaldt*, as mistakenly written by Ugazzi – was a financial figure in Liechtenstein legislation. This asset was entirely suitable for the CMC, because of the *Anstalt*'s ideal qualities: almost zero rules and close to total anonymity. In this notable principality and European fiscal paradise, tiny Vaduz was headquarters of both Miami and Famaco (yes, also that *De* in front of Famaco, after my verification, was a little mistake by Ugazzi). But what my investigation also reveals, is that Famaco was founded on March 11, 1961 and notably survived until 2005, meanwhile Miami remained active until June 20, 1977. That said, the papers I obtained actually show the brilliant journalist was totally right in writing about the presence in the CMC of the Hans Seligman-Schurch & Co. But here again there is something that I can add, and it is that the owner of this bank himself, Hans Seligman, was part of CMC Board of Directors. But more on this later. Going back instead to Capocotta, *Paese Sera,* in a subsequent article, stated: [28]

[We know] about plots of land in Capocotta «sold» to numerous political and military figures and influential civil officers.

The first clues to understand exactly what the newspaper meant are in the inverted commas around the word "sold" as much as in the headline itself: *Lotti di terreno in regalo ai membri del C.M.C.* (Plots of land given as **gifts** to C.M.C. members [emphasis added]). This indicates not a real sale but concessions at prices so highly favorable as to qualify as gifts. This is a trick frequently used to disguise the transfer of bribes and therefore, corrupt activities. In fact, if someone obtains something of value not by paying a reasonable price but for a ridiculously small sum, he is apparently only making a purchase whereas, in reality, the money unpaid is an undercover bribe.

Note that the Italian newspaper made its assertions very probably based on a source inside the CMC itself: the Christian Democrat

---

[28] PAESE SERA: Mario Ugazzi, *Rivelazioni dell'on. Ceravolo sulla organizzazione di cui faceva parte Clay Shaw. Lotti di terreno in regalo ai membri del C.M.C.*, March 12, 1967

member of the Italian parliament Mario Ceravolo, who, regretting his links with the fake business organization, had typed on his own headed notepaper a message to *Paese Sera*. It puts a distance between him and the CMC from the opening lines. It reads: [29]

Mr. Chief Editor,
I refer to the article on the Clay Shaw case which appeared in your newspaper on 4 March 1967. My name was mentioned in it.
To avoid any misunderstandings, misconceptions and false interpretations, I would ask you to publish the following:
I have resigned as a Board member of Centro Mondiale Commerciale as of June 25, 1962 because it was not possible to know the origins of incoming sums gathered abroad by Mr. Giorgio Mantello, and the true destinations of them.

But it is in the closing of the letter that Ceravolo adds:

Nor does it show that I accepted gifts of land plots for development that were offered to me on the Capocotta estate, being already the property of groups and companies derived from Centro Mondiale Commerciale, who were reporting to Giorgio Mantello.
I remain open to any eventual requests for clarification.
Thank you.

(Mario Ceravolo)

Ceravolo's remaining open for clarification is what makes one think that it was he at the source of the scoop that *Paese Sera* made in November 1967. It obtained documents about Capocotta and, thanks to these, revealed the names of those involved, starting with De Lorenzo.

THE CANADIAN ARCHIVE FINDINGS

But before talking of De Lorenzo, *Paese Sera* first of all had explained that the Great Puppet master of this speculative operation

---

[29] A photo of this letter is on *Paese Sera*, March 12, 1967

was the previously mentioned Giorgio Mantello; actually Georges Mandel, before Italianizing his name. Here it is, in fact, what the newspaper wrote about:

[Mantello] in recent months [...] visited America twice, where it seems he found new finances for his activities and above all to conclude the business that he has been doing for years: the purchase of Villa Ada and the Capocotta estate owned by the Savoia heirs. Mandel is a good friend of the Count Pier Franco Calvi di Bergolo, one of the heirs of the ex-king and convinced him not to break up the property, as the other heirs would wish, but to keep it all together until he, Mandel, in a few days will be able to buy it all at great price.

A point, this, on which today we have the fortune to have new revelations which endorse, support and magnify what the newspaper said. More in detail, these revelations come from the positive stubbornness of a researcher, Maurice Phillips, who decided it was necessary to see what was inside the thirty-one boxes that Louis Mortimer Bloomfield, founder of Permindex, had donated just before his death in 1984 to the Library and Archives Canada. Phillips knew perfectly well that Bloomfield himself had expressed the condition that nothing would be opened until twenty years after his death. So, when 2004 came, he was convinced that he would have access to all that Bloomfield deposited. But he was prevented by the decision of Bloomfield's widow, Justine Stern Bloomfield Cartier, to disobey her husband's last wishes. Phillips however, did not give up, and actually went to court, managing to see inside some of the boxes, finding documents which prove, to all effects, that they were accessories to the attempted speculation of Capocotta. Starting from the letter by Bloomfield on 1 April 1959 [30] which shows Bloomfield's personal participation in the operation. But it is not the only

---

[30] From *The Permindex papers II, The unknown Permindex story: Canadian attorneys, Venezuelan corporation and French Rothschild*, published by Phillips on his blog on May 16, 2010

Canadian finding on the CMC-Permindex attempt to speculate. Another one, equally dramatic, is the message by Moe Pascal, Bloomfield's brother-in-law, to both Giorgio Mantello and his son Enrico Mantello, who was also present among the members of the CMC. It reads:

MONTREAL, Que., October 23rd, 1959

Messrs. George and Enrico Mantello,
Rome, Italy.

Gentlemen:

I am enclosing herewith draft in the sum of Fifty-Seven Thousand Dollars ($ 57,000.00) United States Currency, representing payment on account of an interest of Seven and One-half Per Cent (7½%) acquired by myself and my brother, Max Pascal, in the Marina Reale Corporation.

[...]

Yours very truly,

_____

Moe Pascal

Also, in the Canadian archives there is another equally important letter in which Bloomfield explained why the Savoias had trusted the management of business related to their property. Here it is: [31]

a curiously personal and exceptional situation between Mantello and the Royal Family, (inter alia, (a) he financed the Queen Mother in Switzerland during their entire stay when they were completely penniless; (b) he organized and financed the expedition which rescued Count Calvi, the King's brother-in-law, just prior to his scheduled execution; and (c) he is a 33rd Degree Mason with the closest connections in the highest aristocratic circles).

_____

[31] From *The Bloomfield-Rothschilds link. A few more documents*, published by Phillips on his blog on April 25, 2010.

The thirty-third is the final step on the Freemasons' hierarchical ladder. Concerning Count Calvi, his exact full name was Giorgio Carlo Calvi di Bergolo: he was the husband of Jolanda Margherita di Savoia. Jolanda was the first-born daughter of Vittorio Emanuele III and sister of Umberto II, last King of Italy before the country changed from a monarchy into a Republic. In other words, Louis Bloomfield is referring to the father of that Pier Francesco Calvi di Bergolo described as a close friend of Mantello by the journalist Mario Ugazzi on *Paese Sera*. The aforementioned escape from Italy to Switzerland was made by Maria José di Savoia, wife of Umberto II, in the aftermath of the Armistice that on September 8, 1943 had ended the alliance between Italy and Nazi Germany. Thanks to Bloomfield's account above, it's then further made evident how false was the very well-orchestrated campaign begun after Mussolini's death and meant to portray Maria José as a kind of *incognito* socialist, or even communist. A deception that did not fool Giorgio Bocca, a journalist who had been a Partisan; this word indicating his belonging to that faction of Italians who fought undercover against Mussolini. Bocca, then, knew what he was talking about when, at the end of January 2001, on Maria Josè's death, he wrote in the Italian newspaper *La Repubblica* how frankly ridiculous it was to describe her as the "red queen" supporter of the antifascists. To prove it, Bocca recalled Maria José's acquaintance with a figure we already know as a totally ruthless enemy of Marxism: Edgardo Sogno. It means that Maria José was an intimate friend of someone who was, as we have seen, a close companion of the CMC member Giuseppe Piéche. A relationship, this between Sogno and Pièche, that went back, as already explained, to the subversive project named *Pace e Libertà* financed by Allen Dulles. Also consider, besides, that Sogno was a Freemason and member of P2. Coincidently, the only son of Umberto II and Maria José joined P2 as well. Returning to the acquaintance between Sogno and Maria José, a fundamental expect of that was for sure a plan narrated by the right-wing historian Arrigo Petacco. This latter described it in his book *Regina. La vita e i segreti di Maria José di Savoia* (Queen. The Life and Secrets of Maria José of Savoia), writing that:

It consisted in transforming Sardinia into a kind of autonomous kingdom, reigned over by Maria José, while awaiting the turnout of the dynastic situation. Since the island was traditionally linked to the Savoia house, Sogno was certain that his plan would have ignited the spirits of the young Sardinians and enabled the formation of groups of fighters ready to move onto the mainland. He planned to conduct the princess by plane over Sardinia where they would both have jumped out with parachutes.

The idea, continued Petacco, particularly attracted the princess who had no qualms about the parachute, and indeed, when recounting it, used the expression "I found the idea very attractive". She then added that Sogno was very confident of the psychological and practical results of such a *coup*. It is worth noting that this *liaison* between Maria José and Edgardo Sogno was established at almost the very same time in which the friendship between Maria José and the afterwards member of the CMC Mantello arose.

Given such a hugely significant and precise validation, it is even more important to read closely what *Paese Sera* published in November of 1967. After laying hands on documents, the newspaper uncovered all the details of the Capocotta construction speculation, [32] beginning with the date of its origins: 1958. This was the same year that CMC was founded in Rome – further proof of how Capocotta was all part of the shady intentions of CMC. But these documents confirm not only the involvement of the Savoias, but also reveals its astonishing extension: in fact, there was the count Pier Francesco Calvi di Bergolo, very active, as we have seen, as a go-between

---

[32] PAESE SERA: Alfonso Testa, *I grossi nomi dei lottizzatori*, November 8, 1967; see also STAMPA SERA: Luca Giurato, *Forse Capocotta salvata in extremis dalla distruzione*, November 9, 1967

with the CMC; then there was Giovanna di Savoia, daughter of Vittorio Emanuele III and sister of Umberto II; there were the Princes Maurizio, Enrico, Ottone, and Elisabetta d'Assia, all four children of Mafalda di Savoia, sister of Giovanna and Umberto II. But in the Capocotta papers that *Paese Sera* obtained, another royal house appears: that of the Princes of Liechtenstein. It means, exactly the upholders of that tiny nation wedged in between Austria and Switzerland and place of two financial institutions behind *Centro Mondiale Commerciale*. But the speculation papers also found the presence of many CMC members. Besides Mantello, there were, in fact, also the aforementioned banker Hans Seligman, as well as another CMC member: Gaetano Rebecchini. This latter was an Engineer, reason why he was the technical planner of the speculation. Rebecchini's project, fortunately aborted, should have been as follows: 1,100 acres of woods along 2.5 kilometers of coastline, home to deer, wild boar, pheasants, roes and woodcocks, to be chopped down; a natural feature and beauty spot which was considered a unique example of surviving native coastal woodland in Italy, to be destroyed. And for what? To build 1,800 villas, three hotels, golf courses, tennis courts, polo fields, a motorboat dock, seven swimming pools, a stable and riding school, plazas and even a church.

But that behind this speculation there was a bribery is clearly shown by the fact that among those caught up in the speculation was also Admiral Giuseppe Pighini, a top naval officer under fascism and later a high-ranking military figure in NATO, appointed head of *ComNavSouth*, commanding southern Europe's naval forces. And the findings of another Italian parliamentary commission, that on P2 member and *mafioso* Sindona, relate that, according to witnesses, Pighini's name was on a very special list. Special because it was a list of over 500 extraordinarily powerful people who were financed by Sindona. It is worth remembering that Sindona, recruited by OSS agent Max Corvo, was linked to CMC. And on April 1, 1981 the Italian *Commissione d'inchiesta su Sindona* (Commission of inquest on

Sindona) called as witness Carlo Bordoni. Bordoni, a close long-time associate of Sindona, testified that Pighini received millions of dollars from Sindona, deposited in a secret account in the *Amincor Bank*, a Swiss bank owned by Sindona. The reason was to establish an authoritarian military government coup. [33] What a coincidence. Michele Sindona, when questioned about this by the *Commissione Anselmi*, attempted to deny it, but he could not avoid admitting the existence of very cordial meetings between his family and that of Giuseppe Pighini. Finally, last but not least, it is worth recording what was confessed just before his death by the very close associate of CMC member Pièche: Edgardo Sogno. [34] That is Pighini's participation in one of Sogno's seditious projects. As we shall soon see, this subversive attempt includes the name of a CMC member: Corrado Bonfantini, whom I have already mentioned briefly as an associate of Sindona.

But the list of the highly significant beneficiaries of Capocotta is not finished. It also included Gaetano Piccolella, at that time Police Commissioner of Rome and, from 1995 to 1997, the national vice-chief of Italian Police. Piccolella stumbled into an inquiry called Phoney Money, led by the public prosecutor's office in the town of Aosta. [35] But despite having plenty of overwhelming evidence, this inquiry was forcefully stopped by enemies of the prosecutor. How wrong this dismissal of the case was, is certainly shown by a series of events that followed years later: through wire-tapped telephone calls, some of the former inquiry defendants were heard describing schemes which are startlingly similar to the mechanisms of P2.

---

[33] ITALIAN DOCUMENT: *Commissione parlamentare d'inchiesta sul caso Sindona e sulle responsabilità politiche e amministrative ad esso eventualmente connesse. Relazione di minoranza dell'On. Giuseppe D'Alema e altri*

[34] Aldo Cazzullo, *Dalla Resistenza al golpe bianco. Testamento di un anti-comunista*

[35] LA REPUBBLICA: M. P., *Caso Phoney Money. Sentito Maccanico*, May 12, 1996; *'Phoney Money'. Il ministro Flick manda gli ispettori*, December 6, 1996. ADNKRONOS: *Phoney Money: trovati legami con la massoneria internazionale*, July 23, 1996

Phoney Money also accused Pier Francesco Pacini Battaglia, a name linked to the investigation on the *Strage di Ustica* (Ustica Massacre), an event in 1980 which led to the deaths of all the passengers on a flight of the airline company Itavia. Pacini Battaglia's links with Ustica came about through his company Mediterranean, which conducted categorically unusual geological explorations following the plane crash, and precisely in that area of sea where the plane sank after being hit by a missile. The Mediterranenan company had the very interesting characteristic of having exactly the same notary as the CMC.

But there is another final name that comes up from the Capocotta speculation, and it is, as I mentioned, that of Giovanni De Lorenzo. That is to say, he, who at that time, was at the top of an astonishingly powerful Italian intelligence branch known as SIFAR.

WALTERS – DE LORENZO – KARAMESSINES

Why is it so important to focus on De Lorenzo? Because, thanks to this general and Freemason, in 1962 the CIA concluded an agreement with SIFAR against Kennedy. This agreement was in addition to the already existing pact between the CIA and the Freemasons. As stated earlier, it would be impossible not to link the date with the words of the Freemason Milone, spoken during the *Sacro Collegio del Rito* on December 5, 1981, and concerning the risk that Anselmi deciphered in every part of the job against JFK by *Grande Oriente*:

Everything happening [today] has its matrix in what occurred in 1962.

This pact between SIFAR and the CIA had the following guidelines: [36]

Point 1. Program diverse actions for possible emergency situations.

---

[36] Faenza, *Il malaffare*

Point 2. Intensify finances to the forces which oppose the political swing [to the left].

Point 3. Support single leaders in the Christian Democratic Party (DC) and political lobbies willing to rally around the new President of the Republic Antonio Segni (Segni, like Gronchi before him, placed full trust in General De Lorenzo), who did not like the party's opening to the left.

Point 4. Support any action which seeks to weaken the structure of the Socialist Party and favor any kind of internal split.

Point 5. Strengthen voices in the media who are able to influence public opinion in the field of economics and politics.

Segni, actually, was elected President of the Republic in 1962. There is that date again.

Clearly, what the far-right wanted to destroy was JFK's patient and long-sighted attempt to reach an agreement with Moro's DC party: the terms for a government which would include the presence of socialists. In short, the so-called *Apertura a sinistra* (Opening to the Left). [37] It was a task undertaken mostly by one of JFK's main collaborators, Arthur Schlesinger Jr., who relied on the support of the Italian left-wing intellectual Tullia Zevi, his dear friend. [38] This opening had already found opposition in the State Department, a fact which Schlesinger comments on: [39]

By this time it was evident that, if those in State who wanted to block the *apertura* had their way, they might well bring into power a right-wing government with fascist support, like the disastrous Tambroni government of 1960, and force the democratic left into a popular front.

---

[37] Schlesinger, Jr., *A thousand days. John Fitzgerald Kennedy in the White House*; Alan Arthur Platt, *U.S. policy toward the 'Opening to the Left'*; Brinkley, Griffiths, *John F. Kennedy and Europe*; Faenza, *Il malaffare*; Spencer M. Di Scala, *Renewing Italian Socialism. Nenni to Craxi*; Leo Wollemborg, *Stars, stripes and Italian Tricolor. The United States and Italy, 1946-1989*; CRITICA SOCIALE: Stefano Carluccio, *Quel pomeriggio a casa di Tullia Zevi. Il Psi accetta la NATO*, May 2007

[38] Schlesinger, Jr., *A thousand days*; CRITICA SOCIALE: Stefano Carluccio, *Quel pomeriggio a casa di Tullia Zevi. Il Psi accetta la NATO*, May 2007

[39] Schlesinger, Jr., *A thousand days. John Fitzgerald Kennedy in the White House*

However, besides that of the State Department, another voice of dangerous dissent started to be heard, even more risky and irrational. It was that of Vernon Walters, the then US military attaché in Rome, proclaiming the necessity, in the event of socialists in the Italian government, of a US military occupation of the country. [40] This outburst was obviously unacceptable for Kennedy, prompting him to remove Walters, replacing him with the more suitable Colonel James P. Strauss. In any case, as he left, Walters not only kept silent about the agreement reached with De Lorenzo but he even secretly appointed the task of keeping it alive to Thomas Karamessines: an act that bore all the marks of high treason. [41] The latter was later to become a protagonist alongside Kissinger and Nixon, of the US support in Pinochet's *coup* in Chile. [42] This of course left the necessity of finding a secret Italian contact person for Karamessines, and it fell, predictably, to a name also linked to the CMC: Renzo Rocca.

CROCCO, MEMBER OF CMC AND OF THE AMERICAN WAR MACHINE

Rocca was then head of a special branch of the *SIFAR* named *Ufficio REI*. That said, let's go on to look at the case files concerning another of the massacres carried out under the *Strategy of Tension*: eight dead and one hundred and two injured by a fascist bomb detonated in 1974 in Brescia, a northern Italian city. Among these files what stands out is a reserved Report written by Rocca on September 12, 1963, and sent to the P2 member Giovanni Allavena, who was then head of counter-intelligence. Rocca informed him that to bring about "an efficient, serious and global anti-communist

---

[40] Faenza, *Il malaffare*
[41] De Lutiis, *Storia dei servizi segreti*
[42] See, e. g., *White House, Memorandum of conversation, Dr. Kissinger, Mr. Karamessines, Gen. Haig*, October 15, 1970

action in Italy" an amoral approach was needed. It had, therefore, license to abandon all the limits that, on the contrary, no nation should *ever* breach. In fact, Rocca, with no qualms, writes:

We must create a group of activists, young people, teams that can use all methods, even unorthodox, of intimidation, threats, blackmail, street battles, assault, sabotage and terrorism.

To show that it was not simply a theory but a concrete plan, Rocca, a few pages later, makes a list of real people with these subversive ideas, showing, in particular:

activities already taking place which are reported to notable politicians (the organization of Senator Eugenio Reale, the parliamentarian [Randolfo] Pacciardi, the parliamentarian [Alfredo] Crocco, the parliamentarians Scelba and [Guido] Gonella, the parliamentarian Andreotti and other politicians of the following parties: D.C. – P.R.I. – P.S.D.I – P.L.I. – M.S.I.).

The point is Alfredo Crocco was a CMC member too, the documents I finally got reveal. A position certainly earned thanks to his family ties; starting with his father, Arturo Crocco, who was a world pioneer in military aviation technical-scientific progress, having created systems allowing bombs to be dropped so efficiently that they became a pillar of the fascist war forces. That is why Arturo Crocco was given management positions by the dictatorship at both the Air Force Ministry and the National Economy Ministry. This road between science and military aviation was also quickly followed by one of Alfredo's brothers, Luigi, a constant and highly efficient collaborator of his father. So, when the Cold War begun, generating a struggle to bring on board the most capable minds, Donovan, head of OSS, sent one of his best men, Moe Berg, to Italy, to contact Luigi Crocco and his right-hand man Antonio Ferri. The result was that both Ferri and Luigi Crocco moved to the USA, obtaining citizenship and becoming a very significant duo in the area of the US war rockets. [43] However, Luigi Crocco's relationship with his home-land never finished. On the contrary, he boasted permanent very strong ties with the aviation branch of FIAT. [44] This is extremely interesting, because the Agnelli-owned giant was headed in that era by Vittorio Valletta, a secret and prolific financer of both Edgardo Sogno and Renzo Rocca. Not only that but, under Valetta, the chief project manager of FIAT aircraft was Giuseppe Gabrielli, employed in the firm since 1931, having been distinguished for developing jets for the Nazi-fascist forces. Gabrielli was the husband of Lidia Crocco, and therefore, brother-in-law of Luigi Crocco, [45] father of the G-91 fighter plane that won a NATO commission in the 1950s, resulting in the production of 800 planes G-91 as a means of attack of the North Atlantic Treaty. [46] This victory was achieved also thanks to pressure in his favor by Theodore von Kármán, a Hungarian physicist who, just like Luigi Crocco and Antonio Ferri, had ac-quired American citizenship. [47] Von Kármán was president of a special NATO structure for the coordination of scientists with the highest contributions to the Western war machine: AGARD. The Italian representative of AGARD was Gabrielli. [48] The pressures are unsurprising when you know that, right from the fascist era, Theodore von Kármán had a very warm acquaintance with both Crocco and Giuseppe Gabrielli. [49] So, the Croccos had powerful

---

[43] See Giovanni Caprara, *Storia italiana dello Spazio*; J. C. Ruiz Franco, *Werner Heisenberg y Moe Berg, dos vidas cruzadas por la incertidumbre*. On Berg and Ferri only: Nicholas Dawidoff, *The catcher is a spy*

[44] Michelangelo De Maria, Lucia Orlando, *Italy in Space*

[45] Giovanni Caprara, *Storia italiana dello Spazio*; Michelangelo De Maria, Lucia Orlando, *Italy in Space*

[46] Giovanni Caprara, *Storia italiana dello Spazio*

[47] Stanley Hooker, Bill Gunston, *Not much of an Engineer*

[48] Giovanni Caprara, *Storia italiana dello Spazio*

[49] Giovanni Caprara, *Storia italiana dello Spazio*; John David Anderson, *The airplane, a history of its technology*; NASA, *NASA's contributions to aeronautics, Vol. I*; see also LA REPUBBLICA: Salvatore Falzone, *L'ingegnere nisseno che rivoluzionò l'aeronautica militare*, November 27, 2015

ties with a character whose connections with the nerve center of the military system of the North Atlantic Treaty were amplified for having created, apart from AGARD, also the RAND Corporation, a fanatically anti-communist think-tank responsible, together with the Pentagon, for the most senseless USA war escalation. [50] It is now totally clear why the CMC member Alfredo Crocco appears in that disturbing letter by Renzo Rocca. Letter that, it should be underlined, went back to only a couple of months before the assassination of JFK in Dallas. It means the ambush for which, as we know, Garrison incriminated the likewise member of the CMC Clay Shaw.

But a close inspection of what Rocca wrote allows us to establish even other elements that fit the picture. To explain what I mean, I will begin by saying that among the paradigmatic events of the struggle between JFK and the power apparatus that wanted him dead, what stands out without doubt is what happened on the brink of a WWIII about to break out due to the discovery of Soviet missiles in Cuba in 1962. While John and Bob Kennedy attempted to prevent an apocalyptic catastrophe at all costs, CIA agent William Harvey, unknown to both, created an operation to further increase tension inside the Caribbean island. Discovering the deception, RFK was quick to rail against Harvey. As perfectly recounted by RFK Jr., son of Bob Kennedy: [51]

In direct disobedience of a presidential directive, Bill Harvey, the CIA's bug-eyed, gun-toting, Cuba project director dropped sixty elite commandos into Cuba to prepare the ground for the invasion they deeply hoped would follow. My father went through the roof when he learned of this act of insubordination in the midst of the hair-trigger missile crisis. "You were dealing with people's lives, and then you're going to go off with a half-assed operation such as this?" he exclaimed. A

---

[50] J. Samaan, *The RAND Corporation (1989-2009)*
[51] RFK Jr, *American values*. See also FAIR PLAY MAGAZINE: Christopher Sharrett, *The Assassination of John F. Kennedy as Coup D'Etat*, May-June 1999. See also: Select Committee to Study Governmental Operations, *Alleged assassination plots involving foreign leaders*, November 1975

defiant Harvey replied, "We wouldn't be in this jam in the first place if your brother had had the balls to invade." A Harvey protector, CIA Deputy Director Richard Helms, realized he had to beat my father to the punch and transfer Harvey out of Washington. Harvey ended up in Italy, where the insubordinate spy continued to mingle with mobsters and plot against the Kennedys. [...] When the House Select Committee on Assassinations (HSCA) investigated the JFK assassination in 1977, investigators considered [the CIA Cuba Operations chief David Atlee] Phillips and his then boss, William Harvey, as central suspects in Jack's murder.

The point is that from his forced exile in Rome, Harvey schemed and formed alliances with – look carefully – De Lorenzo, Rocca e Sindona. [52] In other words, he surrounded himself with three people linked to the CMC. But in reality, we should say four people, since Andreotti, too, was involved for sure because of his role of principal Italian political protector of Sindona. It is worth remembering that Andreotti was cited in Rocca's letter to Allavena alongside the CMC member Crocco. Letter that we will now realize was in reality linked to Harvey too. In fact, previous to its drafting up, Rocca had had a secret meeting exactly with the American. A meeting in which Harvey offered him a list of names of the far-right which he kept in his own safe in the CIA station in Rome. The goal Harvey wanted to reach through this was that of creating together with Rocca a team of individuals "capable of killing, placing bombs and firebombs, and promoting propaganda". [53] These words clearly echo those of Rocca in his subsequent letter to Allavena. So, to sum up: what Rocca sent to Allavena was a document that, in reality, was doubly signed. Next to his own clearly visible signature was Harvey's disguised one. If things weren't already shocking enough, it gets more so seeing that one of the figures Rocca contacted as soon as he heard the American's plea, was actually Valletta, and then Luigi Cavallo, close collaborator of Sogno. But together with Valletta and Cavallo, Rocca

---

[52] Roberto Faenza, *Il Malaffare*
[53] Roberto Faenza, *Il Malaffare*

hurried to contact another character: Valerio Borghese. [54]

The latter was a high official of Mussolini of particular ferocity, having been a commander of a special fascist military unit known as $X^a MAS$. Not only that, but as we will see in a few pages, Borghese had much to do with someone busy providing necessary finances to organize the ambush which killed JFK. But Borghese also had a strong link with the CMC: Corrado Bonfantini. And Bonfantini, in the 1970s, saw his name stand out concerning CIA intrigues, as Italian spy documents certified Bonfantini belonging to an organization linked to a subversive project headed by – here he is again – Edgardo Sogno: that organization was the *Comitati di resistenza democratica* (Committee of Democratic Resistance). And Sogno was supported in this enterprise by US President Nixon's full endorsement, while locally he was supported by the industrialist Eugenio Cefis and also – pay attention – Sindona, [55] Harvey's friend. It is worth restating that we previously met Sindona both through Max Corvo and through the Admiral Pighini fully involved with the CMC concerning Capocotta. And it no less worth restating that Pighini was also involved in subversive fascist operations headed by Sogno, which included an infiltration into the then up-and-coming terrorist left-wing gang: *Brigate Rosse* (Red Brigade). This infiltration was orchestrated by a certain Roberto Dotti, an ex-communist, who then, just like Bonfantini, went on to be a double-agent and one of Sogno's trusted men. So much so, that Dotti was among the founders of *Pace e Libertà* in 1953. [56] This was the same *Pace e Libertà* which was led by Sogno and the future CMC member Pièche, as we know.

Paradoxically, however, Sogno's support by Nixon became the Achilles' Heel that destroyed the project. At that moment, Nixon

---

[54] Roberto Faenza, *Il Malaffare*
[55] Sergio Flamigni, *La sfinge delle Brigate Rosse*; Sergio Flamigni was also kind enough to give me documents showing the links between the CRD and Bonfantini
[56] Sergio Flamigni, *La sfinge delle Brigate Rosse*

found himself forced to make the sensational resignation caused by the colossal scandal of his own making known as Watergate. But this resignation was also inevitably fatal for Sindona, because Nixon was his principal American ally. From then on, Sindona precipitated into an endless series of economic overturns and, as he tried to resolve them, he asked for help from Bonfantini. That is what Rodolfo Guzzi, Michele Sindona's close accomplice, unequivocally declared to the magistrates. Guzzi explained clearly and repeatedly that Sindona, in trying to put his economic empire back on its feet, spared no blackmail or threat, carried out personally by CMC member Bonfantini. [57] Unfortunately, we have to say it was a well-motivated choice. In fact, Bonfantini had already shown himself, since the end of WWII in Italy, as an individual totally unscrupulous and completely at the service of the US right-wingers. In describing this, it leads us back to the commander of the $X^a MAS$, Borghese. It is a trail worth following because, as we will see, it takes us straight afterwards to the passage of the money used to kill JFK. Let's proceed.

BONFANTINI: A DOUBLE-AGENT FOR AMERICAN INTELLIGENCE.

As Nazi Germany was approaching surrender, Bonfantini became a pain in the neck for a man who, in 1978, would become the most popular and loved President of the Italian Republic, and the most internationally renowned: Sandro Pertini. The pair were both Partisan comrades, but with the difference that Pertini was a man of integrity while Bonfantini was a double agent. Bonfantini's double-crossing game caused him to deliver to Sandro Pertini a letter from Mussolini which proposed a deal between fascists and socialists. This pact was *apparently* to ensure the establishment of

---

[57] ITALIAN DOCUMENT: *Commissione Parlamentare P2, Doc. XXIII n. 2-quater, Vol. I, Tomo IV*

a new Northern Republic in the Italian peninsula. A new Republic governed together by fascists and socialists able to resolve their ideological differences and unite themselves in the name of a greater good: patriotism. *Apparently* because, obviously, it was an extreme attempt at keeping fascism alive at all costs. Benito Mussolini himself would confess to it, for example in the secret meeting of March 31, 1945 with the Nazi ambassador Rudolf Rahn. In this get-together, the *Duce* explained that the real aim was a double one: first, to break the unity of the *Comitato di Liberazione Nazionale* (National Liberation Committee) which was a collective of all anti-fascist armed forces; but at the same time, infiltrate democratic lines with a network of fascists. [58] It was surely a well-thought-out plan, but Pertini saw right through it. He immediately tore up the letter, crying out against making deals with dictators. This was the start of a conflict between Pertini and Bonfantini which would last for years, reverberating even in articles Pertini himself wrote for *Avanti!,* the news-sheet of the *Partito Socialista Italiano* (Italian Socialist Party); occurring on April 30, 1947; and once again, with greater force, on 27 January 1949. In these writings, Sandro Pertini said he repeatedly ordered Bonfantini to sever all contacts with representatives and intermediaries of the *pseudo* Republic of Salò. The discussion came up again in this snippet of an interview from 1985 with one of the top leaders of the Italian Communist Party, Giancarlo Pajetta: "We thought Bonfantini was an adventurer. He had odd contacts with the republicans. He had been captured and he had won back his freedom in mysterious circumstances. Actually, we didn't like him." The historian Giuseppe Murgia also refers to this in his work, writing: [59]

When the "Matteotti" [partisan] brigades captured [the fascist] General Graziani, Sandro Pertini opposed the American officer [Emilio Quincy] Daddario

---

[58] See Frederick Deakin, *Storia della repubblica di Salò*
[59] Murgia, *Il vento del Nord*

who wanted to take the prisoner himself, and he ordered that the head of the `army of Salò be shot in compliance with the orders of the Liberation Committee against fascist criminals. But Bonfantini prevaricated and saved him by agreeing with the OSS agent who had taken delivery of the general. Along with Daddario, Bonfantini also collaborated to save the Corporations Minister Angelo Tarchi.

This means the very same Emilio Daddario that during WWII was, once again not by coincidence, direct emissary of Allen Dulles when Dulles, not yet at the top of the CIA, was already in the fore-front of spy activities in Switzerland. [60] But it means also the very same Daddario who, in that very same period, was side by side with Max Corvo. [61] The same Corvo linked to Sindona. And, finally, it means the very same Daddario also engaged in backdoor dealings with the aforesaid Cefis. [62]

But Bonfantini was even an accomplice to the intelligence op-eration that saved the high-ranking fascist Valerio Borghese in ex-change for Borghese being given the role of secret conniver in the NATO espionage. The historian Luigi Cipriani reconstructs the case, beginning on March 8, 1945: as the fascist regime was collaps-ing, Captain Giuseppe Polosa went to Bonfantini, telling him that Angleton of the OSS and Carlo Resio, an Italian naval captain al-ready working as James Angleton's agent under the code name Salty, wished to meet Borghese. Bonfantini informed Borghese immedi-ately. And so it was that Borghese, four days later, in US military uni-form, escorted by Angleton, Resio and another prominent Italian spy called Federico Umberto D'Amato, left Milan for Rome. [63]

---

[60] Richard Smith, *Oss. The secret history of America's first Central Intelligence Agency*; Salva-tore J. LaGumina, *The Office of Strategic Services and Italian Americans*

[61] Corvo, *OSS in Italy, 1942-1945*; Franco Giannantonio, *L'ombra degli americani sulla Resistenza al confine tra Italia e Svizzera*; Piero Messina, *Onorate società*; LA REPUB-BLICA: Ezio Costanzo, *Uno 007 in Sicilia*, July 20, 2010

[62] ITALIAN DOCUMENT: Tribunale di Venezia, Interrogatorio di Eugenio Cefis al ma-gistrato Carlo Mastelloni, December 29, 1995

[63] Read Massignani, Greene, *Il principe nero*; Also: Casarrubea, *Lupara nera*; very useful is also Angleton's interview given to EPOCA: *Valerio Borghese ci serviva*, February 11, 1976.

Proof of this *liaison indigne* between Bonfantini and Borghese abound, starting with Borghese's diary, in which he notes Bonfantini's visits to him. But confirmation that Bonfantini acted to save Borghese is also in the recount of Luciano Barca, top member of the Italian Communist Party. [64] And there is nonetheless the recollection of Edmondo Cione, one of Mussolini's trusted advisors in trying to set up the cunning tripwire Mussolini hoped to trap the socialists with. Cione declared that Bonfantini confided personally that he had been to Gargnano in Lombardy for talks with Mussolini. [65] Moreover, the fascists Mino Caudana e Arturo Assante wrote in their book *Dal regno del Sud al vento del Nord* (From the Kingdom of the South to the Wind of the North) about how Bonfantini fraternized easily with Mussolini's minister Carlo Alberto Biggini as well as with Renzo Montagna, Mussolini's chief of police.

Besides, Alberto Bettini, the fascist police commissioner of Milan, closely witnessed Bonfantini along with a staunch Mussolini supporter called Gabriele Vigorelli. Bonfantini and Vigorelli were physically side by side pleading to resurrect the fallen fortunes of the Republic of Salò by placing it under command of a ruling council formed of right-wing socialists and fascist *camicie nere* (blackshirts). [66]

In effect, there are traces of the plan to form a new government cabinet with Mussolini still in charge and with, among his ministers, Bonfantini and Borghese. [67] But also proof of the *longa manus* of Angleton in favor of Borghese is very evident. First of all, there is an

---

On Resio and Angleton only, see Holzman, *James Jesus Angleton, the CIA, and the craft of Counterintelligence*; Casarrubea, *Lupara nera*; Casarrubea, Cereghino, *La scomparsa di Salvatore Giuliano*

[64] Barca, *Cronache dall'interno del vertice del PCI*
[65] Pier Giuseppe Murgia, *Il vento del Nord*
[66] Stefano Fabei, *I neri e i rossi*
[67] Stefano Fabei, *I neri e i rossi*

interview in 1976 given by James Angleton himself to the Italian weekly magazine *Epoca*, containing the explicit admission of having effectively saved Borghese in 1945 because – Angleton explained – "I was never interested in Borghese's political ideas". [68]

But more than the interview, it is the documents obtained from the excellent Italian historian Giuseppe Casarrubea which speak the loudest. These documents unequivocally demonstrate Angleton's single-minded decision to prevent Borghese from paying the heavy price for crimes committed under the dictatorship. Angleton explains in the document that the aim was indeed to exploit Borghese as an agent in the service of NATO interests. Actually, Borghese got through in the end with a farcical trial in a courthouse presided over by a judge, Paolo Caccavale, who was a man of obvious repute. [69] Caccavale, in fact, had not only been nominated Grand Officer of the Kingdom of Italy in December 1941 thanks to an impulse of Mussolini, but he had also been, since 1937, part of the executive board of the *Unione fascista fra le famiglie numerose* (Fascist Fellowship Among Large Families). [70] It was a body presided over by a certain Gian Giacomo Borghese, a former fascist hierarch and governor of Rome, as well as a close relative of Valerio Borghese. And so it was that Valerio Borghese, safe and well, was able in 1970 to captain a fascist *coup* under the direct command of Angleton.

BORGHESE AND THE PASSAGE OF MONEY TO KILL JFK

But let's leave this *coup d'etat* for later. It would be more opportune now to discuss a liaison established much earlier than the *coup:* that between Borghese and a very odd bank, *Credito commerciale*

---

[68] EPOCA: *Valerio Borghese ci serviva*, February 11, 1976
[69] See Pier Giuseppe Murgia, *Vento del Nord*; Giuseppe Gori Savellini, *Giornalismo del dopoguerra*
[70] ITALIAN DOCUMENT: Gazzetta Ufficiale del Regno d'Italia - N. 299, December 28, 1937; Supplemento ordinario alla Gazzetta Ufficiale - N. 306, December 30, 1941

e industriale (Commercial and Industrial Credit), whose name is often abbreviated to *Credicomin*. [71] Its peculiarity comes from the fact it was embroiled in a chain reaction which led to the killing of John Kennedy.

We should start by saying that at the beginning *Credicomin* belonged to Sindona; the same Sindona who was linked with both Max Corvo and CMC. From here, *Credicomin* landed precisely in Borghese's hands, placing him at its head. When? Early in 1963. [72] And how does this handover from Sindona to Borghese take place? Everything began through the *Società finanziaria italiana*. (Italian Financial Company). It was the SFI who bought the bank from Sindona. The financial company, we should be careful to note, was an out-of-proportion galaxy in which "dozens and dozens of companies gravitate, internationally active in extremely diverse sectors, from agriculture to energy, from information to food, even to real estate." What is more, these labyrinth-like galaxies were dedicated to "high risk investments, lacking any economic logic" along with "falsification of accounting documents to the end of mystifying the reality of assets, […] until money was taken from companies." [73] In other words, it was the usual and perfect channel for murky financial operations.

In the same vein, on the SFI Board of Directors sat two equally sleazy characters. The first was Antonio Cova, brother-in-law of the Christian Democrat Member of Parliament Gronchi. Gronchi, as we will see, was linked to CMC members. The second was Alfonso Spataro, a *Credicomin* member. He was as well the son of another

[71] L'ESPRESSO, Mario Scialoja, *I soldi: da dove venivano, chi li procurava*, November 10, 1974; LA STAMPA: Silvana Mazzocchi, *Giro d'affari internazionale curato da Antonio Lefebvre*, February 19, 1976; DIE ZEIT: H. F. Millikin, *Die Millionen des Diktators*, December 2, 1966; Gianni Flamini, *Il Partito del golpe*, Vol. I; see also AMANECER, *Prosigue el proceso de Gil Robles*, April 12, 1973
[72] Documents in my hands
[73] See Umberto Ambrosoli, *Qualunque cosa succeda*

Christian Democrat Member of Parliament: Giuseppe Spataro. This latter was connected with Felix Morlion, a member of the Dominicans, the religious order. [74] And Felix Morlion was linked to the US spy network and to the Unorthodox war against Communism. [75] In fact, already in 1940 Felix Morlion had founded in Portugal the *Organizzazione cattolica europea anti Comintern* (European Catholic Organization Anti-Comintern), before spending a long period of time in New York where he had been invited by Donovan, the head of the OSS. After this, Morlion established a close relationship with James Angleton and Italian neo-fascism. This led to him initiating and heading the *Università Pro Deo* (Pro Deo University) in Rome, which, apart from being a place of study, was really the secret HQ of Vatican intelligence. Not only that but Morlion's personal secretary was Giulio Andreotti. [76] It means, I repeat, the same Andreotti listed by Renzo Rocca together with the CMC member Alfredo Crocco. Alfredo Crocco whose scientist brother was recruited by Donovan. From here, in an extraordinarily swift chain of events, the SFI became involved in an equally extraordinary consortium made up of The Holy See, the rightest wing of the *Democrazia Cristiana*; Julio Muñoz Cuesta, of *Opus Dei*. A consortium in which there was also Gil Robles, a fervid sympathizer of *Opus Dei*. Robles, moreover, had a very sinister past. In the 1930s, when he had been Minister of War, he had facilitated the military careers of both the despot Franco and also Emilio Mola, a general renowned for his ferocious extra-judicial executions of communists. This presence of *Opus Dei* means a direct participation of the Spanish dictatorship. In fact, from 1957 *Opus Dei* gained a total predominance in the regime, consolidated by the

---

[74] Sergio Flamigni, *La Banda della Magliana e il delitto Pecorelli*; Sergio Flamigni, *Le Idi di marzo*

[75] Gianni Flamini, *Il libro che i servizi segreti italiani non ti farebbero mai leggere*; Cipriani, *Sovranità limitata*; Di Giovacchino, *Il libro nero della Prima Repubblica*; LA REPUBBLICA: Franco Scottoni, *Il pio frate che lavorava per la CIA*, November 27, 1991

[76] Tranfaglia, Casarrubea, *La Santissima Trinità*

entrance of three members of the Catholic sect in the Spanish government: Mariano Navarro Rubio, Laureano López Rodó, and Alberto Ullastres. But within this consortium there was also a series of companies, most of them created by a lawyer, Ovidio Lefebvre d'Ovidio, a name that, decades later, was among the players in the Lockheed Affair. Finally, in this consortium there was also a Central American: Ramfis Trujillo. [77] He was the son of the Dominican dictator Leónidas Trujillo, whose death in 1961 put an end to that dictatorship and forced Ramfis into exile. And where would that exile be? In Spain, of course. It was the time when Allen Dulles's CIA, obsessed with eliminating Castro, had set up secret paramilitary camps in various US locations. They were used to train Cuban anti-communist exiles against Fidel. Well, precisely one of the instructors of those exiles, Gary Hemming, revealed to the newspaper Solares Hill in 2005 the existence of a very notable meeting: [78]

Hemming revealed who he believed were two of the "sponsors" of the assassination. Two men met in Haiti in February of 1963 and contributed funds for the Kennedy assassination. Both were from the Dominican Republic. One, Ramfis Trujillo, an international playboy who dated Hollywood starlets, was the son of long-term Dominican Republican dictator Rafael Trujillo, who was assassinated in May of 1961. The second man was Johnny Abbes Garcia, former intelligence director for General Rafael Trujillo. It was not the first time Garcia had financed an assassination. In 1959, Garcia hired American adventurer Alexander Rorke to smuggle eight men into Cuba on one of the first missions to kill Castro.

In February 1963, at the same time as the meeting described by Gary Hemming occurred, the relationship between SFI and the

---

[77] L'ESPRESSO, Mario Scialoja, *I soldi: da dove venivano, chi li procurava*, November 10, 1974; see also LA STAMPA: Silvana Mazzocchi, *Giro d'affari internazionale curato da Antonio Lefebvre*, February 19, 1976; DIE ZEIT: H. F. Millikin, *Die Millionen des Diktators*, December 2, 1966; Gianni Flamini, *Il Partito del golpe*, Vol. I; see also AMANECER, *Prosigue el proceso de Gil Robles*, April 12, 1973
[78] SOLARES HILL: J. Timothy Gratz and Mark Howell, *The 'Kill Castro' business. From No Name Key to Death in Dallas*, March 11, 2005

consortium headed by Ramfis Trujillo was consolidated. But there was another coincidence in time with another more important and singular event: the conclusion of a whirlwind of activities, bouncing between Swiss banks and a new company, Ventana. These activities brought *Credicomin* into the hands of Trujillo. It was at that point that Borghese became its new president; and, last but not least, a colossal sum of 10 billion Lire (the Italian currency prior to the Euro) belonging to Trujillo, was deposited into *Credicomin*. But it disappeared immediately, and conveniently, into nowhere. [79]

A sign that the link between *Credicomin* and Borghese concealed something else, is traceable in a CIA document of March 9, 1971. When the popular Italian newspaper *La Stampa* wrote about the connection between the bank and the neo-fascist, the then head of the CIA station in Rome urgently alerted the Head of the CIA Division in Europe. [80] Besides, a strong and precise link existed between Borghese and the CMC member Clay Shaw. In fact, when Garrison, the New Orleans DA, arrested Shaw under suspicion of having taken part in the assassination of JFK, he seized Shaw's address books, and found telephone numbers directly dating back to Marcella Borghese, [81] who was Paolo Borghese's wife and a cousin of Valerio Borghese. A fact to which we should add what occurred in 1970 to one of the most respected US prosecutors ever: Robert M. Morgenthau. That year, he was forced to resign. Well, in 2012, Morgenthau revealed that the cause was an ultimatum by the Nixon administration ordering him to stop investigating a Swiss bank account

---

[79] L'ESPRESSO, Mario Scialoja, *I soldi: da dove venivano, chi li procurava*, November 10, 1974

[80] Central Intelligence Agency. Special Collection: Nazi War Crimes Disclosure Act. Document Number (FOIA)/ESDN (CREST): 519a6b27993294098d511210. Borghese, Junio Valerio. Borghese, Junio Valerio 0037. March 8, 1971

[81] U.S. NATIONAL ARCHIVES, Garrison Papers, Clay Shaw's Notebook

belonging to Ramfis Trujillo's father. The point is that the account was created with Richard Nixon's complicity. [82]

The interview in Solares Hill was not the only publication which carried declarations by Hemming about a dark connection between the murder of JFK and Ramfis Trujillo. In 1996, an article in the Kennedy Assassination Chronicles, summarizing what Hemming said to the pioneering JFK-Lancer Conference that same year, had included these two key sentences: [83] "Fund-raising meetings were convened in Port au Prince and attended by [Haiti's dictator] Papa Doc, Trujillo family members, and others." and "In Montreal, Arturo Espaillat gathered funds from Canada and Europe and sent them to Dallas in order to fund a French team." So, in Hemming's words Canada reappears as part of a triangle of funding involving Europe, in perfect accordance with the data before shown on *Credicomin*. Please consider that Hemming did not hesitate to confirm ties between the Haitian tyranny and the assassination of JFK even during a solemn moment. It occurred when he was cross-examined by the House of Representatives Select Committee on Assassinations, [84] which between 1976 and 1978, returned to scrutinize the Dallas shooting. In that place, Hemming stated that in Dallas, a certain Arturo Espaillat, head of Dominican military intelligence during the dictatorship by Ramfis's father, had come from Canada. And, together with Espaillat – Hemming added – there was also Robert Johnson, an American involved in Rafael Trujillo's repressive system. In short, Hemming's account to the HSCA was the latest in a series of how the story of Oswald as a solitary sniper perched in a

---

[82] Amherst College (Mass.), Rand Richards Cooper, *Law and Order in real life*, 2012; see also REUTER: Daniel Trotta and Paritosh Bansal, *Manhattan DA calls Guantanamo national disgrace*, April 10, 2007

[83] KENNEDY ASSASSINATION CHRONICLES: Charles Drago, *Hemming does Dallas*, WINTER 1996, Volume 2, Issue 4

[84] HSCA, Gerald Patrick Hemming's Audition, 3-21-78

book depository waiting to shoot JFK was only a red herring, artfully constructed.

CMC AND THE CARCANO OF DALLAS

In fact, if we dig deep enough about the Carcano, the rifle that Oswald allegedly used, we come once again across elements that are fully in tune with a conspiracy involving the CMC. The *Carcano* is an Italian-made weapon. In fact, Carcano is nothing more than the surname of the Italian technician who designed the product. Like any rifle or pistol, even the Carcano linked to the Dallas shooting was legally required to carry a serial number: C2766. [85] Through this number, it is possible to find out its precise history, going back to a name: Samuel Cummings. During the 1950s, Cummings was a member of Adam Consolidated Industries, a company based in two locations, New York and Rome, and dealing in the sale of arms. [86] Well, after checking through an Italian intelligence document, we discover he is the same Samuel Cummings trustee of Enrico Frittoli. [87] And who was Frittoli? As yet another Italian Intelligence document shows, he was a close acquaintance of Licio Gelli. [88] And if we look further into Adam and the *Carcano*, two more particular presences emerge. The first is SIFAR, the Italian military espionage at the center of the pact against Kennedy by the Freemason General De Lorenzo. The same De Lorenzo so keen on the United States and the CMC. The second is Andreotti. SIFAR's hand is seen in a cablegram sent by J. Edgard Hoover, head of the FBI, to Rome on June 10, 1964. It speaks explicitly about a SIFAR report, which contains

---

[85] *The Warren Commission report. Appendix X. Expert testimony*
[86] See George Thayer, *The war business*
[87] ITALIAN DOCUMENT: Commissione parlamentare d'inchiesta sulla Loggia massonica P2. Allegati alla Relazione. Doc. XXIII, n. 2-quarter, Vol. VII, Tomo XI
[88] ITALIAN DOCUMENT: Commissione parlamentare d'inchiesta sulla Loggia massonica P2. Allegati alla Relazione. Doc. XXIII, n. 2-quarter, Vol. VII, Tomo XI

detailed information about the famous shotgun. [89] We can link that with a dispatch from Harvey, head of the CIA station in Rome, and dated December 31, 1963, which states that the report was written on demand by Giulio Andreotti and overseen by the same. [90] So, once again, here is the Andreotti listed in Rocca's letter together with the CMC member Crocco. The same Giulio Andreotti who was an intimate associate of Morlion, at the core of Vatican intelligence. Morlion who appears in a photo together with CIA agents and the member of parliament Giuseppe Spataro. It means the very same Giuseppe Spataro father of Alfonso Spataro, a member of the Board of Directors of *Credicomin* and *Società finanziaria italiana* (Italian financial company) through which the transfer of money between Trujillo and Borghese took place at almost the same time as Trujillo's Haitian travel to raise the necessary funds for the assassination of JFK. Furthermore, the *Carcano* in question was part of a surplus army stock from WWII. Left over from the fascist Army, it ended up among a pile of re-conditioned arms stock in a bid which Adam awarded. [91] The bid was announced by the Italian Ministry of Defence in 1960. And who was the minister in 1960? Giulio Andreotti, of course.

And yet still, the Adam company, in order to sell off the arms stockpile which included the *Carcano*, used Crescent Firearms. The *factotum* of Crescent was Joseph Saik, a Ukrainian and fervent anticommunist who, at the same time, was at the head of Adam. [92] Joseph Saik, above all, during WWII had been part of the American Headquarter in France directed by Dwight E. Eisenhower. [93] And

---

[89] FBI Warren Commission Liaison File (62-109090), FBI 62-109090 Warren Commission HQ File, Section 13

[90] Oswald 201 File (201-289248). NARA Record Number: 104-10019-10008. *Italian Report on Type of Rifle used in JFK Assassination*, June 10, 1964

[91] LIFE: Keith Wheeler, 'Cursed gun'. *The track of C2766*, August 27, 1965

[92] LIFE: Keith Wheeler, 'Cursed gun'. *The track of C2766*, August 27, 1965

[93] Obituary in *The Ukrainian Weekly*, March 28, 1982

one of Eisenhower's closest collaborators at that point was General Charles Thrasher. Coincidentally, he was the same Thrasher whose *aide-de-camp* was the CMC member Clay Shaw, as Shaw himself admitted in an interview for the monthly magazine Penthouse. [94] For Shaw, it was his first foray into the world of Intelligence. Thrasher, actually, was part of an OSS branch known as SOS, which stood for Special Operations Section, [95] and whose objective was "all organized Federal espionage and counterespionage operations outside the United States and its possessions for the collection of foreign intelligence information required for the national security. [… Duties that] may involve semi-overt and semi-covert activities for the full performance of the mission". [96]

Shaw reappeared in a Memorandum, Garrison's Charges Against the CIA, dated September 15, 1967, and declassified only in 1999. It states that Shaw worked for the Agency, and that one of his duties was to spy on South American countries. [97] Indeed, Shaw spied on the Argentine Peròn and his wife Evita, further papers prove. [98] But other evidence show that Shaw also spied against East Germany. [99]

But a CIA memo also reveals that Clay Shaw was in a program of the Central Intelligence Agency called QKENCHANT, which also

---

[94] PENTHOUSE, James Phelan, *An exclusive Penthouse interview: Clay Shaw*, November 1969

[95] Mellen, *A farewell to Justice*

[96] Central Intelligence Agency. *Organization and functions of the Office of Special Operations Section I general*, June 6, 1947 Document Number (FOIA)/ESDN (CREST): CIA-RDP78-04007A001000030032-3,

[97] CIA. HSCA. Segregated CIA Collection, (microfilm - reel 25: Garrison, Agrupacion Montecristi - DRE), *Garrison's charges against Cia*, September 15, 1967. NARA Record Number: 104-10170-10156

[98] CIA. *Information Report: Political influence of Juan Pistarini*, June 29, 1951. NARA Record Number: 104-10276-10449

[99] CIA. HSCA. Segregated CIA Collection, (microfilm - reel 17: Ruiz - Webster) Reel 17, Folder G - CLAY SHAW, *Information Report: Directory of Firm in International Trade*, March 20, 1952. NARA Record Number: 1994.05.09.10:43:33:160005

included Monroe Sullivan. [100] It was the same Sullivan who provided Shaw with an alibi placing him far away from the events in Dealey Plaza, Dallas, on November 22, 1963. [101] But another document testifies that the CIA had someone else in mind for the QKENCHANT project: Guy Banister. [102] He was another protagonist of the Garrison inquest in 1967. And Banister's involvement in QKENCHANT is even more astonishing when we know that witnesses questioned by the Select Committee on Assassinations of the U.S. House of Representatives referred to a collaboration between Banister and the law office of a certain G. Wray Gill. This was in the autumn of 1963; so, therefore, very close to the assassination of JFK. The aim was to help the mafia boss Carlos Marcello fight a court case against Robert Kennedy. In helping Marcello, Banister was flanked by a certain David Ferrie, a close associate of Clay Shaw; so close that he was also questioned by Garrison, who indicated he too was involved in the assassination. [103] Finally, QKENCHANT also included CIA agent Howard Hunt. [104] This was the Hunt who, on his deathbed, admitted

---

[100] CIA. HSCA. Segregated CIA Collection (microfilm - reel 30: Mexico City Station File). *Memo. Subject: Clay L. Shaw (201-813493).* NARA Record Number: 104-10195-10007; CIA. HSCA. Segregated CIA Collection, Box 45, *Sullivan, Monroe J. (J. Monroe) Subject claimed to be with Clay Shaw in San Francisco all day on 22 November 1963*, NARA Record Number: 104-10255-10016

[101] CIA. HSCA. Segregated CIA Collection, Box 45, *Sullivan, Monroe J. (J. Monroe) Subject claimed to be with Clay Shaw in San Francisco all day on 22 November 1963*, NARA Record Number: 104-10255-10016; CIA. HSCA. Segregated CIA Collection (microfilm - reel 30: Mexico City Station File). *Memo. Subject: Clay L. Shaw (201-813493).* NARA Record Number: 104-10195-10007

[102] CIA. HSCA. Segregated CIA Collection, Box 40. *Memorandum. Subject: Request for Special Inquiry - Guy W. Banister Associates New Orleans.* NARA Record Number: 104-10109-10374

[103] Appendix to Hearings before the Select Committee on Assassinations of the U.S. House of Representatives. Vol. X; see also National Archives, Jim Garrison Files, Banister, Guy

[104] HSCA Segregated CIA Collection, Box 43, Memo: Hunt working for Publishing Company, June 3, 1970. NARA Record Number: 104-10119-10323; HSCA Segregated CIA Collection, Box 43. Security File on E. Howard Hunt. NARA Record Number: 1993.07.24.08:35:20:900310

that the CIA had killed Kennedy. And many accounts exist on Hunt, including that of his own son Saint John, about his own involvement in the plot to assassinate JFK in Dallas.

THE BORGHESE COUP

New confirmation of what has been explained up to now can be seen from further events regarding Borghese. In fact, not only was there a relative of Borghese in the address book seized by Garrison from Clay Shaw; not only was Borghese saved at the end of WWII by the OSS member Angleton and future CMC member Bonfantini; not only was Borghese head of a bank linked to Ramfis Trujillo, financier of the shooting of JFK but, even more than all that, in 1970 Borghese led a coup in Italy with another CMC member: Piéche. [105] The coup enjoyed the support of both Angleton and Nixon. Besides, in this *coup* another of Angleton's recruits during WWII participated. It was Licio Gelli, head of that P2 so closely entwined with the CMC.

Licio Gelli's part in the coup is actually proven by audio recordings made by a captain of the Italian Carabinieri (military police), Antonio Labruna. The coup failed, and in order to save Gelli from the legal consequences he deserved, Andreotti stepped in, in a way very similar to how he had already covered up the investigation into the *Carcano*. These are the details, as recounted to the Italian judge Guido Salvini who had made extensive inquiries on the facts: [106]

At the end of July [1974] a meeting took place in the private office of the parliamentarian Giulio ANDREOTTI, then pro-tempore Minister of Defence. [...].

---

[105] Giannuli, *Il Noto Servizio*
[106] ITALIAN DOCUMENT: *Sentenza-ordinanza del Giudice Istruttore presso il Tribunale Civile e Penale di Milano, dr. Guido Salvini nei confronti di AZZI Nico ed altri*

The minister had been brought the tapes of the interviews with [Remo] Orlandini [107] at Lugano and the transcripts and probably too, a draft of the report drawn up by Colonel Romagnoli [...].
The parliamentarian Andreotti, at the end of the meeting, advised the leaders of the S.I.D. to "bury the loot" [...].

To be explicit, burying the loot means that Andreotti demanded that most of the tapes recorded by Labruna be destroyed. The group obeyed, cancelling any reference to Licio Gelli, including the links between the coup and two people connected to Nixon: Pier Talenti and Hugh Fenwick. [108] The involvements of Talenti and Fenwick apart from the aforementioned tapes, are confirmed also by Italian Intelligence reports. [109] Fenwick, by the way, had evident links with the CIA, proven by a document of January 1951, [110] which was not only declassified after 50 years but, even today, contains censored portions. As for the association between Talenti and Nixon, here is what Tim Weiner in his One Man Against the World: The Tragedy of Richard Nixon writes:

Illegal and unreported funds started flowing into the campaign [of Nixon] during September and October 1968. Nixon had learned through his associations with the CIA and the FBI during his years under Eisenhower that suitcases stuffed with cash were instruments of foreign policy for an American commander in chief. He now applied the methods of covert operations to obtaining campaign contributions.
One source of his clandestine cash was the military junta in Greece. Its leaders were pleased by Nixon's surprising choice of a running mate, the governor of Maryland, Spiro T. Agnew, born Spiros Anagnostopoulos, raised in the Greek Orthodox Church. The junta contributed $549,000 to the Nixon campaign through

---

[107] Orlandini was connected to neo-nazis and Nixon
[108] ITALIAN DOCUMENT: *Sentenza-ordinanza del Giudice Istruttore presso il Tribunale Civile e Penale di Milano, dr. Guido Salvini nei confronti di AZZI Nico ed altri*
[109] ITALIAN DOCUMENT: Commissione P2, Doc. XXIII D. *2-quarter, Vol. III, Tomo IV, Parte I*
[110] Central Intelligence Agency, General Collection, Document Number (FOIA)/ESDN (CREST): CIA-RDP80R01731R003000270033-8, *Letter to Mr. Hugh Fenwick from (SANITIZED)*, December 18, 1951

Thomas Pappas, a Boston businessman who ran the largest oil company in Greece. Pappas was a personal friend to Nixon and the colonels; he became known in the White House as "the Greek hearing gifts."

A coalition of right-wing leaders in Italy served as another source of covert contributions to Nixon. They kicked in hundreds of thousands of dollars through Pier Talenti, an Italian American industrialist with fascist tendencies and a vast family estate in Rome. Nixon himself instructed his chief of staff, H. R. Haldeman, to help handle "this contribution from the Italian." Nixon liked to reward his contributors when he could: as president, he personally approved millions of dollars in covert support to right-wing Italian politicians through the CIA and tens of millions in weapons sales to the Greek colonels through the Pentagon.

Weiner returns to the subject of Talenti even in his acclaimed Legacy of Ashes. It reads:

The [Central Intelligence] agency had secretly supported politicians in Western Europe throughout the cold war. The list included [...] every Christian Democrat who ever won a national election in Italy.

The CIA had spent twenty years and at least $65 million buying influence in Rome and Milan and Naples. [...]

Nixon and Kissinger revived that tradition. Their instrument was the CIA's Rome station and the extraordinary ambassador Graham Martin.

Kissinger called Martin "that cold-eyed fellow" [...] No American diplomat was more deeply enamored of covert operations.

Nixon thought he was terrific. "I have great personal confidence in Graham Martin," he told Kissinger on February 14, 1969, and with that, the machine was in motion.

Martin's appointment as ambassador in Italy was the handiwork of a wealthy right-wing American named Pier Talenti, who lived in Rome, where he had raised hundreds of thousands of dollars for the 1968 Nixon campaign among his friends and political allies. That opened the door to the White House. Talenti went to see Colonel Alexander M. Haig, Jr., Kissinger's military aide, to deliver a warning that the socialists were on the verge of taking power in Italy and a proposal that a new American ambassador was needed to counter the left. He named Martin, and his message went right to the top. Martin had persuaded Nixon and Kissinger that "he was just the man, because he was tough as nails, to bring about a shift in Italian politics," said Wells Stabler, his deputy chief of mission in Rome.

Richard Gardner, USA ambassador to Italy from 1977 to 1981 adds: [111]

I had another negative experience with the American Embassy in the period from 1969 to 1972, when Graham Martin was President Nixon's ambassador in Rome. […] [D]uring my visits to his office in the Rome embassy, he railed against American critics of Nixon's Vietnam policy as "Communists" and seemed to believe a Communist takeover of Italy was imminent. Martin relied for advice on very conservative Italians such as Michele Sindona, a corrupt financial manipulator, and Paul Marcinkus, whose unwise financial transactions were to cause a crisis in the Vatican Bank. He was also profoundly influenced by an extreme right-wing Republican Party representative in Italy Pier Talenti. Martin avoided relations with political leaders, but he devised a secret program to finance centrist and ultra-right-wing politicians, about which I shall say more later. This program was revealed by congressional investigations and further damaged America's reputation in Italy.

And also, speaking during a symposium: [112]

When I arrived in Italy in March of 1977, America's reputation in Italy was at an absolute low point. I didn't make that point too starkly in the book, because one doesn't like to criticize too much one's predecessors, but I'll say it to an audience like this. It was not just the result of the Vietnam War and Watergate, and the assassination of the two Kennedys and Martin Luther King. What the United States had been doing in Italy in the previous eight years under Nixon and Ford was unforgivable. Graham Martin, who was ambassador from 1969 to 1972, poured vast amounts of money into the pockets of right-wing politicians, including the head of the secret services of Italy, a well-known neo-fascist, who was later implicated in a plot to take over the country by force, by somebody named Prince Borghese, a real right-wing nut. The other major influence on Graham Martin was a man named Pier Talenti, a great friend of Nixon's, a Nixon fundraiser, who was an Italian-American who lived in Italy. He was brought to trial by the Italian government for implication in this subversive plot.

---

[111] Gardner, *Mission Italy. On the Front Lines of the Cold War*
[112] Gardner, *My Italian Mission: Ethical dilemmas and lessons for today*, Carnegie Council for Ethics in International Affairs, January 19, 2006

The Freedom of Information Act is a wonderful thing. All these things come out now. They brought out recently a document in which Pier Talenti came to see Alexander Haig and said, "The Communists are about to take over Italy. We've got to corrupt some more politicians." That was how they wanted to combat communism.

Gardner's statement is certainly to be considered in the light of another document, this one sent to Henry Kissinger. It is a cable-gram from Graham Martin, at that time ambassador in Rome, and, once again, also this is only partly declassified. In it, Martin praises Pier Talenti, emphasizing how he had been very useful in establishing enormously valuable contacts with sectors of the Italian far-right. [113] This was easy for Pier Talenti, seeing as he was the nephew of Achille Talenti, building constructor and founder of the firm *Tudini e Talenti*, together with Giuseppe Tudini, that had given rise to an entire neighborhood in the north-east of Rome in the 1960s. Well, a further document from the CIA, dating from the postwar period, unmasks both Tudini and Talenti as financers of Borghese's neo-fascist activities. [114] There is more: Talenti was the brother-in-law and spy operations partner of Herbert Itkin, [115] an informer who was closely connected to the FBI and CIA. It is extremely interesting to note a declaration by Itkin. Recruited by the CIA in 1954, he had been contracted straightaway, by direct order

---

[113] Central Intelligence Agency, Library of Congress Collection, Document Number (FOIA)/ESDN (CREST): LOC-HAK-165-5-6-7, *Cable to Henry Kissinger from Graham Martin*, December 1970
[114] Central Intelligence Agency, General Records, Document Number (FOIA)/ESDN (CREST): CIA-RDP82-00457R000300660008-2, *Monarchist and Right Wing Movements. Neo-Fascist Movements*, date unknown (probably, 1947)
[115] CIA, HSCA segregated CIA collection, box 38. *Itkin's story of his work for Cia, as related from notes by Warren Donovan.* NARA Record Number: 104-10107-10116; CIA, HSCA segregated CIA collection, box 38. *Chronology re to Itkin.* NARA Record Number: 104-10107-10125; CIA, HSCA segregated CIA collection, box 38. *Exerpts relating to Itkin assertions.* NARA Record Number: 104-10107-10100; CIA, HSCA segregated CIA collection, box 38. *Itkin, Herbert - Assertions.* NARA Record Number: 104-10107-10101

of Allen Dulles, to George de Mohrenschildt. [116] The latter was a right-wing Russian and featured among the key figures in the assassination of JFK. Despite being a millionaire, he was inexplicably a friend of the scapegoat Lee Oswald. Also, he had worked for a company, Three States Natural Gas Co., [117] belonging to D. Harold Byrd, [118] who, despite also being a millionaire too, was furthermore the one who had rented out to the Texas School Books Depository the building in Dallas which Oswald had been accused of shooting from on November 22, 1963. [119] I will explore this fact later on in greater detail.

The relationship between Mohrenschildt and Herbert Itkin certainly lasted throughout the 1960s, a fact undoubtedly interesting also because of another precise detail: Mohrenschildt's involvement in a CIA operation which took place in 1963 in Haiti, and known by the codename WUBRINY. [120] That is to say, at the same time and place when Ramfis Trujillo was sent to sort out the necessary money and organize the shooting of JFK. Trujillo's mission to Haiti was simultaneous – I once again emphasize – to a highly relevant and mysterious transfer of money by the Dominican through a bank headed by none other than Borghese. An astonishing synchronicity that nonetheless emerges in seeing that Itkin too was at that time similarly employed by the CIA in Haiti, in activities which involved the local organized crime and whose principal goal was to

---

[116] NEW TIMES MAGAZINE: Dick Russell, *Three witnesses*, June 24, 1977. See also: Dick Russell, *On the trail of the JFK assassins*

[117] CIA, Russ Holmes work file: *Col. Lawrence Orlov: educational and professional record*, NARA Record Number: 104-10431-10034; WC, Warren Commission Hearings, George S. De Mohrenschildt

[118] TEXAS STATE HISTORICAL ASSOCIATION: Jerrell Dean Palmer, *Byrd, David Harnold*, June 12, 2010. See also: Dick Russell, *On the trail of the JFK assassins*

[119] Richard Bartholomew, *Byrds, planes, and an automobile*

[120] CIA, Russ Holmes work file: *Contact Report: A meeting was held in the library of the knickerbocker*, April 25, 1963. NARA Record Number: 104-10436-10014; CIA, HSCA segregated CIA collection: *Contact Report WUBRINY Haitian operations*, April 25, 1963. NARA Record Number: 104-10070-10076

"harass Cuba, if not invade it, from the northwest part of Haiti." [121] It means it was a part of the US's attempt to bring down Castro. This makes it impossible to ignore what is noted by many scholars of the JFK affaire, first and foremost Garrison: [122] the CIA operation against the Cuban president would transform, at a specific point in time, into a mission to kill John Kennedy. This, because the CIA knew that if a successful way to kill JFK existed, it was certainly to conceal this plot inside another already planned plot. A transformation that, while Itkin was intent on his so special Haitian mission, was for sure already accomplished. And with whom Itkin made his mission in Haiti? With none other than Talenti, as well as another significant figure: Mario Brod. [123] He was significant because Brod had been a US spy agent since 1944 when, like Gelli and Borghese, he had been personally recruited by – once again – Angleton. [124] The bond between Mario Brod and Angleton remained eternally solid. So much so that in 1962 Mario Brod, together with Angleton, handled the case of the KGB deserter Anatoly Golitsyn. [125] Golitsyn's declarations in the USA after his defection inspired morbid adoration in Angleton, given the Russian's harmony with the top CIA official's pernicious paranoia. Like, for example, when the delirious Russian accused almost all the heads of the western world of being sold out to the soviets.

---

[121] CIA, HSCA segregated CIA collection, Box 38, *Transcript of tape #1 re Itkin, Herbert*. NARA Record Number: 104-10106-10321

[122] NBC TV NETWORK: *Jim Garrison's declaration about his own investigation on JFK Assassination*, July 15, 1967

[123] CIA, HSCA segregated CIA collection, Box 38, *Excerpts relating to Itkin assertions*. NARA Record Number: 104-10107-10100; CIA, HSCA segregated CIA collection, *Staff notes*. NARA Record Number: 180-10143-10196; CIA, HSCA segregated CIA collection, Box 38, *Transcript of tape #1 re Itkin, Herbert*. NARA Record Number: 104-10106-10321; CIA, HSCA segregated CIA collection, Box 38, *Transcript of tape #2 re Itkin, Herbert*. NARA Record Number: 104-10106-10322

[124] CIA, HSCA segregated CIA collection, *Staff notes*. NARA Record Number: 180-10143-10196

[125] Valentine, *The strength of the wolf*

But James Angleton – please, pay attention – turned up nonetheless exactly inside the attempted coup in Italy in 1970, starting with the support given to that act by the P2 member Federico Umberto D'Amato, [126] since the Italian was one of the Angleton's best fellows, as demonstrated by the fact that it was D'Amato the one who at the end of WWII helped Angleton in getting Borghese's rescue. Elements that easily explain what a classified paper traced by the Italian judge Casson shows: D'Amato was also a CIA agent. [127] Besides, the Italian magazine *L'Espresso* revealed on February 8, 1976 how Angleton arrived in Italy a few weeks prior to the coup, then left abruptly following its failure.

To complete the puzzle, Borghese, in a sort of testament written just before his death, actually named Angleton as the principal supporter of the coup. [128] The testament made enthralling reading. After being hidden for thirty years, it was finally delivered to the Italian judiciary in November 2003. It called Pier Talenti into play. Also, it offered an excellent explanation as to why the subversive coup failed. At the last moment, the news was leaked to top officials in the Italian Communist Party. This explanation matches facts given by the most notorious informer of Cosa Nostra of all time, Tommaso Buscetta. In November 1992, Buscetta explained that the countermand arrived when the Soviet fleet positioned itself dangerously close in the Mediterranean. [129] So, basically, the coup had been stopped to avoid a Third World War. Coincidentally, Buscetta knew that, exactly like Talenti's Haitian operation, the coup also involved the mafia. Not

---

[126] ITALIAN DOCUMENT: *Sentenza-ordinanza del Giudice Istruttore presso il Tribunale Civile e Penale di Milano, dr. Guido Salvini nei confronti di AZZI Nico ed altri*; see also: Sergio Flamigni, *Trame atlantiche*
[127] Sergio Flamigni, *Trame atlantiche*
[128] ITALIAN DOCUMENT: Procura Della Repubblica Di Brescia. Relazione di Consulenza. Procedimento penale n. 91/97 mod. 21. Provvedimento di Nomina di Consulente Tecnico e Conferimento Incarico dell'11 novembre 2003, Ex Art. 359 C.P.P. al Dott. Aldo Sabino Giannuli
[129] Sergio Flamigni, *Trame atlantiche*

the American mafia obviously, but the Italian mafia, both the Sicilians and the Calabrese. In particular, there was an intermediary between Borghese and the Calabrese mafia (known as the 'ndrangheda) – Paolo Romeo, a lawyer, Freemason and, at the same time, Italian spy agent. [130] In fact, if the news leak, as explained by Borghese, had got as far as the leaders of the PCI (Italian Communist Party), then it was certainly obvious that they had alerted the Kremlin, resulting in the redeployment of Soviet naval ships in the Mediterranean in order to signal that the subversive operation must absolutely end. And it must absolutely end also because of another secret revealed in Borghese's spiritual testament: that if the coup had been successful, the Italian fascist had promised Nixon to send Italian troops to Vietnam, overturning one of the most significant pledges enshrined in the Italian constitution: to not take part in wars. A kind of promise indeed able to enrage Moscow. On the other hand, it is a further highly plausible reason for Nixon's support for Borghese's 1970 coup. He could get help for the war in South-East Asia from which Kennedy instead had actively shown himself willing to withdraw.

THE CMC MEMBER GIUSEPPE ZIGIOTTI

This is not all. Along with the testament, there is a book of notes which amplifies the connections with the CMC. These notes include phrases in which make it clear that among those involved in Borghese's coup was a certain Pier Francesco Nistri. Once a member of Mussolini's Intelligence in the Republic of Salò, Nistri was also responsible for the arrest and shooting of many anti-fascist in Rome during the dictatorship. When fascism collapsed, Nistri entered the *Movimento Sociale*, a political party secretly supported, as we know, by the CMC member Pièche. But Pier Francesco Nistri

---

[130] Sergio Flamigni, *Trame atlantiche*

also became president of a so-called *Associazione Nazionale Combattenti in Spagna*. The point is that this ANCIS was founded by Arconovaldo Bonacorsi in 1949. This latter was a vicious supporter of Mussolini, as his endless shootings of anti-fascists during the Spanish Civil War undoubtedly shows. Note that ANCIS, just like the CMC or Pièche's *Antincendi*, was a cover-up. In fact, behind the disguise of an association for war veterans, it concealed an anti-communist armed force. [131] This is a necessary premise to understand the real intentions of a meeting of fascists in Spain on October 16, 1963. That is to say, a week before Dallas. At the meeting, Nistri met with Arturo Scattini, who was an ex-soldier in Mussolini's intelligence, and with a third man, Giuseppe Zigiotti. [132] Also a fervent supporter of Mussolini, [133] after the war Zigiotti became president of the so-called *Associazione nazionale arma milizia* (National Association of Armed Militia) which was formed, like ANCIS, by veterans of Mussolini's dictatorship. In accordance with the general picture, there is also an inventory of the funds of the *Associazione nazionale dei combattenti della X^a Flottiglia MAS* (National Association of Fighters of the 10th MAS Fleet). This inventory shows that correspondence between Zigiotti and Borghese did exist. [134] Unsurprisingly, Giuseppe Zigiotti was yet another CMC member. Furthermore, there is a really disturbing fact: Nistri's ANCIS involvement at the head of a neo-fascist demonstration precisely the day before JFK's death. The demonstration was supported by the Italian *Movimento sociale* and the Spanish Embassy. Leaving no doubt about its connotations, groups of neo-fascists

---

[131] See Albanese, del Hierro, *Transnational fascism in the twentieth Century*

[132] ITALIAN DOCUMENT: Appunto Sid 2/8132 A-Sismi, *Confederazione Europea degli ex Combattenti, con sede a Parigi. Raduno internazionale a Madrid, Valle dei Caduti,* October 16, 1963

[133] Imelde Rosa Pellegrini, *L'altro secolo. Cent'anni di storia sociale e politica a Portogruaro (1870-1970)*

[134] *Museo Storico Italiano della Guerra* di Rovereto

linked to *Movimento sociale* and called *Formazioni Nazionali Giovanili* (National Youth Formation) had been handing out leaflets all over Rome. The leaflets attacked the center-left which JFK wanted to help create, repeating the exact same accusations presented by William Harvey and the Italian Intelligence against the President. The pamphlets raged that the center-left would lead Italy into a communist dictatorship. They even invoked the rise of a military dictatorship like the one in Spain. [135]

It was all compatible with what later emerged about Nistri and Scattini thanks to the comparison with a SIFAR document of August 12, 1964. [136] The pair, in cahoots with the neo-fascist movement *Ordine Nuovo* (New Order), were both secretly busy identifying soldiers with progressive ideas inside the Italian Armed Forces. We should remember 1964 is the year of the coup headed by De Lorenzo, an enemy of JFK, and that 1964 is also a step away from the publication of a book with the eloquent title *Le mani rosse sulle Forze Armate* (Red Hands on the Armed Forces). Written by Guido Giannettini and Pino Rauti, both neo-fascists who took part in 1965 in that meeting at the Hotel *Parco dei Principi* in Rome which established the rules for the Strategy of Tension. Gianettini was also linked to the Italian espionage. Coincidentally, Rauti was one of the founders of the aforementioned fascist group *Ordine Nuovo*.

But the seminal moment of that *Parco dei Principi* meeting was, in reality, another very special far-right meeting celebrated on November 22, 1961 and opened by a goodwill message from the then NATO Secretary General: Dirk U. Stikker. This 1961 meeting was organized by Randolfo Pacciardi. The same Pacciardi who had an excellent relationship, as the Italian-American Freemason himself

---

[135] Albanese, del Hierro, *Transnational fascism in the twentieth Century*
[136] ITALIAN DOCUMENT: Appunto Sifar A-Sismi, *Visione a Sig. Capo Ufficio*, August 12, 1964.

underlined, with Gigliotti, [137] the CIA man who had arrived in Italy to set up the anti-Kennedy pact thanks to a trip sponsored by the CMC member Giuseppe Pièche. The same Pacciardi who, moreover, as we know, was present, along with the CMC member Crocco, in the list of politicians Rocca indicated as those prepared to use violence in conducting a war against communism. In other words, Rocca's list was a list of politicians ready to use the Strategy of Tension. Besides, this November 1961 summit saw the participation of Italian neo-fascists. One of these was Mario Tedeschi, a P2 member and clearly one of the most relevant brains behind the Strategy of Tension, as reflected in this quote of May 11, 1969, where he said: [138]

We prefer bloody insults to bloodless bombs. Nowadays, to be a true anti-communist, you must place yourself out of the system and against the regime.

Finally, this November 1961 meeting included the very large presence of the Antibolshevik Block of Nations, an organization very much in the sphere of Allen Dulles, and also Richard Nixon. Actually, the Antibolshevik Block of Nations was crucial to the success of two of Nixon's extremely important victories: the one of the Eisenhower-Nixon electoral ticket, and Richard Nixon's own election in 1968 as POTUS. In fact, the ABN was central to the birth of the National Republican Heritage Groups Nationalities Council at the heart of the Nixon administration. It is worth adding that a really predominant role inside the NRHGN was that of the Freemason Philip Guarino. [139] By another extraordinary coincidence, Guarino was linked to Gelli, the head of P2, and to the really relevant P2

---

[137] Central Intelligence Agency, Special Collection, Hillenkoetter Diaries, Document Number (FOIA)/ESDN (CREST): 5166d49399326091c6a604c2, January 3, 1950
[138] ITALIAN DOCUMENT: Commissione parlamentare d'inchiesta sulle Stragi – Doc. XXIII n.64, Vol. I, Tomo III
[139] ITALIAN DOCUMENT: Procura della Repubblica di Brescia, Relazione del 12/03/97 del dott. Aldo Giannuli, a seguito di incarico del 21/01/96 del G.I. MI, *Lega Anticomunista Mondiale, Nuclei di Difesa dello Stato, Aginter Presse, Ordine Nuovo, Fronte Nazionale*

member Sindona. This latter was a close cohort, as we know, of the CMC member Bonfantini.

But there was still a final sensational revelation in Borghese's testament. It was that Andreotti too was in accordance with the coup; to the point that the notorious politician was destined to be the appointed Prime Minister to head the government imposed by the takeover. [140] So, basically, Andreotti had covered everything up to protect himself first and foremost. A cover-up that, in fact, worked perfectly. The legal authorities could not reach any conclusion. That is how Pièche, who had fled to Malta when, as I said, his name appeared among the suspects, was able to return to Italy, his reputation unscathed. [141]

THE MEMORANDUM OF 1948. A PRECURSOR OF THE PLOT AGAINST JFK.

Yes, we go time and again back to Andreotti. Or, rather, to the connecting thread between the assassination of JFK, the Italian and American far-right, the Strategy of Tension and Italian neo-fascism. A thread that somehow unfurls also into the past. Further proof of this is an Embassy Memorandum drafted by Paul Hyde Bonner in 1948. Bonner was then at the head of the US diplomatic presence in Rome. The subject of this Memorandum was not only the creation of a clandestine front against the social-communists, but also a plan to remove the politician who at that time led the DC: Alcide De Gasperi; who needed to be ousted – the document states – because he was considered too lenient with the communists. A plan against Alcide De Gasperi that succeeded and whose analysis is extremely

---

[140] ITALIAN DOCUMENT: Procura Della Repubblica Di Brescia. Relazione di Consulenza. Procedimento penale n. 91/97 mod. 21. Provvedimento di Nomina di Consulente Tecnico e Conferimento Incarico dell'11 novembre 2003, Ex Art. 359 C.P.P. al Dott. Aldo Sabino Giannuli
[141] Giannuli, *Il Noto Servizio*

important to understand the plot against JFK, starting with the fact that, involved in this plot against De Gasperi, were two future CMC members, Angelo Sagna and Giuseppe Azzaretto. That is the reason why they were in fact both cited in the Memorandum by Bonner.

But going in order, we should explain, first of all, the general situation. Since the fall of Mussolini there had been various governments in Italy, all of them characterized by the presence, alongside the DC, of socialists and communists, both parties having proved themselves highly capable of holding key responsibilities and ministries. At that time, the so called *Conventio ad excludendum* had in fact not yet appeared. This was a tacit agreement by all the rest of the forces in the Italian constitution not to allow the left-wing parties to return to power. It was a prohibition whose roots lie in the 1947 meeting between De Gasperi, father and head of the DC, and Truman, and during which the US President gave a firm ultimatum: keep the Marxists out, or no more American money. [142] De Gasperi, hesitant at first about such an extreme step, finally gave in to the *diktat* not least because of the clear message which reached him from Sicily: the *Strage di Portella* (Portella Massacre). This bloodshed in May 1947 of left-wing workers was committed by a Mafia gang headed by Salvatore Giuliano, but behind it all was the CIA, the extreme right of the DC, nostalgic Mussolini supporters, and other future members of the CMC.

But more about Portella later. Now, we should concentrate on another matter: the exclusion of the left by De Gasperi could have been thwarted by the Italian general election of April 18, 1948. There were many signs that the first election in a republican Italy could have given the Marxists a win which would have made them

---

[142] Lepre, *Storia della prima Repubblica. L'Italia dal 1943 al 1998*; Gambino, *Storia del dopoguerra. Dalla liberazione al potere DC*; Castagnoli, *La Guerra Fredda economica. Italia e Stati Uniti 1947-1989*

able to form an independent government without the support of *Democrazia Cristiana*. It was for this reason that, forty days before the votes were to be cast, the National Security Council proposed – obviously, in top secret – Draconian guidelines. They were: [143]

Demonstration of a firm United States opposition to Communism and assurance of effective United States support might encourage non-Communist elements in Italy to make a last, vigorous effort, even at the risk of civil war, to prevent the consolidation of Communist control

Once this has been made clear, it should be added that in Bonner's Memorandum appears Luigi Gedda. He was certainly an *élite* figure inside the Vatican, as his leadership of *Azione Cattolica* (Catholic Action) shows. This position was also certainly the fruit of his anticommunism which was extreme enough to make him capable of anything against the Italian anti-capitalist parties. An anti-communism so strong that it even encouraged Gedda to create a second organization, *Comitati Civici* (Civic Committees), much more prepared and much more aggressive and bolder than *Azione Cattolica*. Gedda managed to strengthen these *Comitati Civici* to as many as 300,000 enrolled members. As the essayist David Teacher recorded: [144]

according to the American Embassy and the CIA representative in Rome, they undertook 'psychological warfare' and were considered by the Embassy to be the most important anti-communist group, which the Embassy felt justified a subsidy of $500,000 from the State Department to the CIA

It was also the reason why the *Comitati civici* actually remained active up until the 1960s. Their true nature was well-outlined in the testimony to the judiciary of Vito Talamini, one of their ex-militants, who spoke about the astounding rate of secret comings and goings

---

[143] National Security Council, S/S–NSC Files, Lot 63D351, NSC 1 Series, *Position of the United States with respect to Italy in the light of the possibility of Communist participation in the Government by legal means (NSC 1/3)*, March 8, 1948
[144] David Teacher, *Rogue Agents*

of hand grenades, rifles, machine guns and pistols thanks to the complicity of parish priests, high-ranking prelates and faithful members of the flock. [145] It all reflected another point in the above-mentioned document of the NSC: [146]

United States security interests in the Mediterranean are immediately and gravely threatened by the possibility that the Italian Communist-dominated People's Bloc will win participation in the government in the April national elections [...]
In the event the Communists obtain domination of the Italian government by legal means, the United States should:
a. Immediately take steps to accomplish a limited mobilization, including any necessary compulsory measures, and announce this action as a clear indication of United States determination to oppose Communist aggression and to protect our national security.
b. Further strengthen its military position in the Mediterranean.
c. Initiate combined military staff planning with selected nations.
d. Provide the anti-Communist Italian underground with financial and military assistance.
e. Oppose Italian membership in the United Nations.

In the Memorandum, Bonner finally cites, as I said, the two future CMC members Azzaretto and Sagna. All this explained, it is now time to outline the astonishing parallels between 1948 and what happened to Kennedy. A passage in the Memorandum states: [147]

Both Sagna and Gedda expressed strong feelings that the D.C. had been weak and vascillating [sic] in carrying on their mandate in order to create confidence among the mass of Italian voters. As Gedda expressed it, the party was like a rudderless ship, drifting here and there on every current.

---

[145] ITALIAN DOCUMENT: Commissione stragi, XIII legislatura, Doc. XXIII n. 64, Vol. I, Tomo II. *Il Piano Solo e la teoria del Golpe negli anni Sessanta*. Elaborato redatto dai senatori Vincenzo Ruggero Manca, Alfredo Mantica e dal deputato Vincenzo Fragalà
[146] National Security Council, S/S–NSC Files, Lot 63D351, NSC 1 Series, *Position of the United States with respect to Italy in the light of the possibility of Communist participation in the Government by legal means (NSC 1/3)*, March 8, 1948
[147] Memorandum of conversation, Paul Hyde Bonner, Rome Embassy, Dinner with Comm. Angelo Sagna, Marchese Origo and Professor Luigi Gedda, October 6, 1948

Therefore, Sagna, despite the then leader of DC giving in to the US order to exclude the left, judged De Gasperi too weak a politician *anyway* for the dictates of the *Guerra non ortodossa* that Sagna was trying to impose. The excellent election results obtained by the party in terms of votes were not enough. Neither were the highly conciliatory words spoken by De Gasperi towards Sagna which transpire in this other passage from the Memorandum:

Sagna stated that he had received indirect word from the Prime Minister through Andreotti that the P.M. was heartily in favor of the plan of Sagna's group to solidify the party along the lines of firm policy in the economic, political and agricultural fields.

If this is what happened to the condescending De Gasperi, it is very easy to understand with what increased virulence the CMC would then apply itself to the destruction of the inflexible JFK regarding the return of socialists in the Italian government.

THE MOVEMENT FOR EUROPEAN UNITY

But two other parallels exist between the situation the Memorandum describes and that which led to the death of JFK. They are the presence of the CIA and dirty money. Bonner writes:

Gedda said that the International Federation of Catholic Action could and would be used for promoting the idea of Western Union. He called attention to an article on the subject in the latest issue of "Collegamento", the organ of the Comitati Civici.

Luigi Gedda here is hinting at something which at high levels in Washington was taken very seriously in those years. The essayist Stephen Dorrill puts it well: [148]

---

[148] Dorrill, *MI6: Inside the Covert World of Her Majesty's Secret Intelligence Service*

American support for Luigi Gedda, a prominent Vatican official who ran 'Catholic Action', a significant force in the 1948 elections, increased when he began to deploy his organization to promote the idea of 'Western Union', explaining that the Pope had agreed that 'the Church should carry the banner for a federation of European states'.

In other words, Gedda promised the USA a European Union under the control of Washington and staunchly anti-communist. In fact, on March 3, 1949, the *Movimento per l'unità europea* (Movement for European Unity) was created, and its administrative secretary was none other than Sagna, the future member of CMC. As for the other members of the MUE, apart from ex-followers of Mussolini's dictatorship there was also the industrialist and senator Enrico Falck. This was the same Falck who featured in a secret American document as being present at a meeting in Turin in June 1945. The meeting was to agree to funds for the anti-communist movements. But besides Enrico Falck, there was a second industrialist present, Vittorio Valletta. [149] And as we know, Valletta was a financier of *Pace e libertà*, the anti-Marxist group set up by Sogno together with CMC member Pièche. And he was also covertly subsidizing Renzo Rocca, who was one of the key figures in that anti-Kennedy pact signed by the CIA and the Italian spy network. And let us not forget that in the time he directed FIAT, Valletta also took under his wing Giuseppe Gabrielli, the link between the powerful Italian motor company and the US military-industrial complex. And Gabrielli was the brother-in-law of CMC member Alfredo Crocco, described in a letter by Rocca as ready to fight the *Guerra non ortodossa* against communism. And Alfredo Crocco's brother Luigi was similarly closely connected to the US military-industrial complex, so much so that he was recruited by Donovan.

---

[149] Casarrubea, Cereghino, *Tango connection*

Coincidentally, Donovan reappears regarding another event concerning one of the characters in Bonner's Memorandum. In fact, in May 1950, Gedda was the go-between in a meeting in the Vatican with the intent of pursuing anti-communist objectives. The protagonists were Pope Pius XII, Giovanni Montini, future Paul VI, and Joseph Retinger, a Polish exile and leader of the European Movement. [150] If we match this event with documents obtained by the historian Joshua Paul, we discover that this European Movement was covertly and massively financed by ACUA; that is, the American Committee for a United Europe, which arose in 1948. And the director of ACUE was specifically William Donovan. And not only that, but the vice-director was Allen Dulles. [151]

But parallels with the circulation of dirty money was made even clearer in a third passage of Bonner's Memorandum. This one:

Sagna stated that all questions of foreign policy within the D.C. should be held in abeyance until Italy had put her own house in order, by which he meant a strong and clear policy with respect to industry, agriculture and trade unions – one that was not dominated by Socialist planning.

Sagna said that he and Azzaretto together had just completed the purchase of all of the shares of Banco di Santo Spirito from I.R.I. I gathered that it was their intention to use the profits from this venture for the benefit of D.C. and such other related needs as might arise. (Azzaretto is the owner of the Societa [152] Martini e Monti of Milan and of Longanesi, the publishing house.)

Sagna cautioned that any contributions made to either Gedda or the D.C. should be made on a monthly basis in order to control the proper use of funds.

Effectively, Monti & Martini – because in the company name the surnames of the co-founders are actually in this order – was a

---

[150] Retinger, Pomian, *Memoirs of an Eminence Grise*
[151] THE TELEGRAPH: Ambrose Evans-Pritchard, *The European Union always was a CIA project, as Brexiteers discover*, April 27, 2016; Ambrose Evans-Pritchard, *Euro-federalists financed by US spy chiefs*, September 19, 2000; DIPLOMACY & STATECRAFT: Richard Aldrich, *OSS, CIA and European Unity: The American Committee on United Europe 1948-60*, March 1, 1997
[152] It should be: Società

chemical industry created by Giovanni Monti, associate of Leo Longanesi in the publishing company of the same name and still in existence today. Monti & Martini passed on to Giuseppe Azzaretto, as Bonner specified, and then on to Longanesi. Anyway, thanks to the Memorandum, we can see how the takeover of the Longanesi company through the takeover of Monti & Martini and *Banco di Santo Spirito* had the purpose of greater and more ominous activities, as well as illegal. Illegal and useful for the objectives of Andreotti. At the dinner at Angelo Sagna's house, Andreotti had already been an informer for United States intelligence for three years, as demonstrated by a document traced in USA Archives with the expertise and patience of the historian Casarrubea. [153]

It is a dispatch of February 20, 1946. His letter shows a Giulio Andreotti so murderously anti-De Gasperi that he blew the whistle across the Atlantic about the contents of classified conversations with the naive Alcide. But as confirmation that the takeover of the Longanesi company concealed something, there exists also a precise testimony by the son of Giuseppe Azzaretto, Dario. In it, Dario Azzaretto talks explicitly about the purchase of Longanesi by his father, adding that it was done with the secret complicity of Pope Pius XII and Andreotti in order to make Longanesi a mouthpiece of anti-communist propaganda. [154] What Dario Azzaretto doesn't say, and what has finally now emerged through the papers of the CMC which I fortunately got my hands on, is that Angelo Sagna and Giuseppe Azzaretto belonged to the CMC. If we then analyze the last sentence of Bonner's Memorandum, we get an even clearer picture of how that dinner at the house of the future CMC member Sagna was the precursor to the intrigue against JFK. The sentence in question concerns a character who, in the light of Bonner's guests, was capable of taking the place of De Gasperi. We read:

---

[153] Casarrubea, Cereghino, *La scomparsa di Salvatore Giuliano*
[154] Gümpel, Pinotti, *L'Unto del Signore*

Sagna said that either the P.M. must show strength and courage or he should be replaced by a stronger man. His idea of a strong man was Gronchi.

Gronchi's support makes it necessary to return to his brother-in-law Antonio Cova. Cova was part of the *Società Finanziaria Italiana* used for the transfer of money to Junio Borghese by Trujillo. The very same Trujillo in that identical period of time intent on financing the murder of JFK. Moreover, Gronchi was President of the Italian Republic from 1955 to 1962, a position granted to him by the Italian parliament. And the member of parliament who managed to get Gronchi elected with the sufficient number of votes by deputies and senators, using all his influence was, of course, Andreotti. And since it is the task of the President of the Republic in Italy to nominate a prime minister, it was therefore Gronchi indebted to Andreotti and two future members of the CMC who made Tambroni premier on March 25, 1960. It is once again useful to repeat: we are talking of a politician whose son-in-law, Franco Micucci Cecchi, was a member of the CMC. And it was Tambroni's government who politically assisted that agreement between the Italian and American Freemasons whose secret end was to fight JFK with any means. In addition, Fernando Tambroni was ready to lead Italy into fascism via a coup which fortunately failed. What I may now attest is that Gronchi was an *accomplice* to that coup. First of all, there exists a very clear note by the then Italian Ambassador to Washington Manlio Brosio. Gathering the comments off-the-record by two other diplomats from his country, Brosio wrote in his diary: [155]

[Fausto] Bacchetti and [Luciano] Conti have told me that the aim was above all to prevent Tambroni's increasing power from taking hold. There was fear of a power grab between Gronchi and Tambroni. Tambroni had already gotten Gronchi to sign the provision declaring a state of emergency.

---

[155] Manlio Brosio, *Diari di Washington, 1955-1961*

And at this point, let's examine what Brosio was forced to admit to the journalist Ugo Zatterin, once the coup had failed. Zatterin had collaborated very closely with Tambroni during the attempted subversion. So, he knew very well what he was saying when he admitted that among the most magnanimous financial donors of the intended coup were "the lawyer Umberto Ortolani, notable businessman" and the Amalfi entrepreneurs from Palermo. "The Amalfis," points out Zatterin, making them out to be the key to it all, "are related to Francesco Cosentino, [...] close personal friend and associate of Tambroni, as well as advisor, together with Professor [Giuseppe] Mirabella, of the President [of the Republic] Gronchi". [156] Cosentino, like Ortolani, was a member of Gelli's P2. Cosentino had a meeting with the then secretary of the US Embassy in Rome Robert Mudd; this in June 1960, when Tambroni was *already* Prime Minister but also he had *already* endured a conflict with the left wing of his party headed by Aldo Moro. The encounter with Mudd was later recorded in a document that first of all confirmed the collusion between Gronchi and Tambroni already mentioned by Zatterin himself. Here is the relevant passage: [157]

There is no doubt that high-ranking people (probably Gronchi and Tambroni himself) wanted favorable comments to come from the embassy to Tambroni. Mr Cosentino has a silver tongue but at the end of the meeting it was clear what his objective was [...].

But Mudd's account revealed the same intention to destroy precisely Moro. It reads:

---

[156] LOTTA CONTINUA: *Finché la banca va – Storia del Banco di Sicilia (1)*, August 2, 1972; Similar statements also in Zatterin's book: *Al Viminale con il morto: tra lotte e botte l'Italia di ieri*
[157] L'ESPRESSO: Gianluigi Melega, *Così parlò Cosentino*, July 28, 1995

Cosentino is Tambroni's man [...]. For the Prime Minister [Tambroni] there is no need to turn to the Psi [Italian Socialist Party], to resolve Italy's social problems [as instead Moro wants to do].

This turns up again later, with words that follow with remarkable similarity the opinion on De Gasperi in Bonner's Memorandum. Let's read:

[Cosentino] complained about the absence of a political leadership in the DC and he made it clear that he considered the secretary Moro as weak. [...] Tambroni, he said, is convinced that the country needs someone who can teach the Italians how to respect authority (Cosentino specified that there is a difference between authority and authoritarianism).

This is a phrase which echoes the power struggle between Gronchi, who was doing everything he could to keep Tambroni in power, and Moro, who instead was doing everything he could to block him. But the conspiracy between Tambroni and Gronchi is rendered even more evident if we go back five years. In 1955, Giovanni Gronchi, still as President of the Republic, insisted and succeeded in making Tambroni Internal Minister. During his time as minister, Tambroni created a secret team, doing illegal activities under the aegis of the CIA. [158] There are various documents to prove it. First of all, a classified Note, linked to the first one above. It is dated May 13, 1959, and was written by Italian Intelligence. It reports on the substantial financial donations, training and technical machinery provided by the CIA to Tambroni's special team. And another Note, linked to the previous one, dated one week earlier, specifies that the supervisor proposed by the CIA for this operation was

---

[158] ITALIAN DOCUMENT: Atti inviati il 23 Luglio 1996 al Giudice Guido Salvini dal RAGGRUPPAMENTO OPERATIVO SPECIALE CARABINIERI Reparto Eversione. Nr.509/62 di prot. "P". OGGETTO: Procedimento penale contro Rognoni Giancarlo ed altri. Annotazione sulle attività di guerra psicologica e non ortodossa, (*psychological and low density warfare*) compiute in Italia tra il 1969 e il 1974 attraverso l'*"AGINTER PRESSE"*

Robert Driscoll. [159] Who was he? He was a pupil of Allen Dulles, as well as the vice-chief of the CIA station in Rome. We should close this argument by outlining how Tambroni's spy team had been camouflaged by an import-export company, a strategy strongly analogous to that of the CMC. [160] Indeed, to summarize the situation: in 1960, under the CMC's protective wing, a double convergent project was unfolding, with multiple aims. They were: to place Nixon in the White House from 1961, to put Moro to one side and to bring dictatorship back to Italy. Fortunately, however, a handful of extra votes placed JFK in the Oval Office, while Tambroni was defeated by the left wing of the *Democrazia Cristiana* led by Moro himself, JFK's great ally.

Keep in mind that a further demonstration of how much all these facts are interconnected with what happened in Dallas in 1963 is also that in 1963 Luigi Gedda, together with another character of the international Right, was co-founder of INTERDOC (International Documentation and Information Center). Naturally, also INTERDOC was an instrument of the CIA to contrast the so-called *Pericolo rosso* (Red Scare), as now declassified US papers can prove. [161] And if we care to complete the examination of Azzaretto's biography, then we come face to face with another deadly lead on the mortal attack of 1963 on JFK, which implicates the member of the *Centro Mondiale Commerciale* Clay Shaw, as we shall see.

MARELLA: THE BRIDGE BETWEEN THE CMC MEMBER AZZARETTO AND DALLAS

---

[159] ITALIAN DOCUMENT: Atti inviati il 23 Luglio 1996 al Giudice Guido Salvini dal RAGGRUPPAMENTO OPERATIVO SPECIALE CARABINIERI Reparto Eversione. Nr.509/62 di prot. "P". OGGETTO: Procedimento penale contro Rognoni Giancarlo ed altri. Annotazione sulle attività di guerra psicologica e non ortodossa, (*psychological and low density warfare*) compiute in Italia tra il 1969 e il 1974 attraverso l'*"AGINTER PRESSE"*

[160] De Lutiis, *Storia dei Servizi segreti in Italia*

[161] David Teacher, *Rogue Agents*

Giuseppe Azzaretto was in fact related by marriage to a distinctly conservative cardinal, Paolo Marella. This latter was the extremely influential personal spiritual advisor to Pope Pius XII whose dark plots are portrayed in Bonner's Memorandum. But the same Marella was coincidentally a protagonist in a secret meeting in August 1966 with one of the most important representatives of the Dallas far-right, the oil tycoon Haroldson Lafayette Hunt. The meeting with Marella had a definite source. In fact, it was the same oil tycoon who recounted in 1969 what the objective was: to beat communism in the world through a forthcoming alliance with the Vatican. [162] The point is that there are many undeniable clues showing H. L. Hunt's involvement right in the middle of the international plot which led to the death of the 35th President of the USA. These clues linking the oil man and JFK's death can be explored starting with page 14 of the *Dallas Morning News*. In fact, on the exact same day that Kennedy was shot, the newspaper asked itself twelve questions, each one more biased than the last. They were printed surrounded by a black border in the funereal style, and tried to portray JFK as a crypto-communist, but not even very cryptic. The hand behind this sinister and very macabre announcement was discovered to be that of Nelson B. Hunt, son of H. L. Hunt. [163] Besides, in the same year, 1963, a very popular radio program was transmitted constantly over the Dallas airwaves. It was called Life Line, and it was a vehicle of continuous and ferocious attacks against Kennedy. Life Line's creator was H. L. Hunt. But H. L. Hunt's path also crossed with that of Jack Ruby, the providential killer of Oswald. Providential because, in this way, Ruby eternally silenced the man who protested he was only a scapegoat. This was for sure a foreshadowing of the truth Oswald wanted to tell – that it had all

---

[162] THE OBSERVER: Jon Pepper, *H. L. Hunts 'Pact' with the Vatican*, March 9, 1969
[163] Manchester, *The death of a President*

been a plot. Press cuttings about Hunt were found in Ruby's possession, as was the telephone number of Lamar Hunt, who, obviously, was another son of the oil man. [164]

So, Paolo Marella met in 1966 with the fascist and sworn enemy of JFK: H. L. Hunt. And Marella was the same relative and sponsor of Azzaretto, a member of that CMC so linked to the Dallas ambush. What a coincidence indeed! And what was this 1966 meeting's aim? This meeting had one objective: a project that was decidedly anti-communist. Not only that, but the project had a very particular location as its headquarters: [165]

The project was now centered in New York, Hunt said, at the Asian Speakers Bureau, with the Free Pacific Association Inc., on Riverside drive.

The Free Pacific Association, Inc. was connected to the activities of the Reverend Sun Myung Moon, leader of a religious cult but secretly connected to the CIA. [166] And aside from H. L. Hunt, Marella and Spellman, there was also a fourth member at the meeting: Father Felix Andrew Morlion. [167] It was the same Morlion who was a close and covert collaborator of the CIA and tight-knit associate of Andreotti, as we know. And it was the same Morlion appearing in a photograph dug out from a weekly magazine called *Mondo d'oggi*, A photo in which he was next to three members of US Intelligence, as well as the politician Giuseppe Spataro who was part of the board of directors of a bank, called *Credito commerciale e industriale*. It means the same bank governed by Valerio Borghese, already a commander of the pro-Mussolini special military unit named X^a MAS. And *Credicomin* was also the bank which, under its ambiguous direction, was occupied in murky dealings with the

[164] David Miller, *The JFK conspiracy*
[165] THE OBSERVER: Jon Pepper, *H. L. Hunts 'Pact' with the Vatican*, March 9, 1969
[166] Betty Clermont, *The Neo-Catholics: Implementing Christian nationalism in America*
[167] THE OBSERVER: Jon Pepper, *H. L. Hunts 'Pact' with the Vatican*, March 9, 1969

Spanish and Italian Right, the Vatican, *Opus Dei* and, lastly, Ramfis Trujillo, son of a Central American dictator. Trujillo, who deposited in *Credicomin* a huge sum which then mysteriously disappeared. And it disappeared right when Trujillo was intently occupied in a tense mission – according to the account of the instructor of anti-Castro mercenaries, Hemming – to organize the funds necessary to kill JFK. What a coincidence, once again!

RFK'S ILL-FATED REFUSAL TO BE HEAD OF THE CIA.

The assassination of JFK that, as in a tragic farce, Allen Dulles was called on to investigate becoming a member of the Warren Commission. The same Dulles, that is, who completely betrayed the trust of JFK to the point that he had been already pensioned off by the end of 1961. [168] It is very clear that the intention to pension him off was in order to totally change the face of the CIA. While he was showing Allen Dulles the door, Kennedy ordered that the authorities and CIA field of action should be drastically reduced. [169]

JFK actually used two Memoranda, issued at the same time on June 28, 1961. Apart from the direct witness account of ex-Colonel Fletcher Prouty, liaison officer between the CIA and the Pentagon at that moment, and nonetheless one of the consultants who helped to draft the outlines of the Memoranda themselves, [170] today we have direct access to those acts. The first, NSAM 55, puts all operations of a warlike nature, even those up to then the prerogative of the CIA, under the control of the military authorities. We read: [171]

---

[168] David Powers, Kenneth O'Donnell, Joe McCarthy, *Johnny we hardly knew ye*
[169] Powers, O'Donnell, McCarthy, *Johnny we hardly knew ye*; Schlesinger, *A Thousand Days; John F. Kennedy in the White House*
[170] Fletcher Prouty, *The secret team*
[171] Department of State, *Foreign Relations of the United States, 1961–1963, Volume VIII, National Security Policy*

The Joint Chiefs of Staff have a responsibility for the defense of the nation in the Cold War similar to that which they have in conventional hostilities.

Given that the Supreme Military Leader is, in the end, actually the President of the United States, it is understandable how, in that way, the final objective of John Kennedy was to have full control of situations which had been up to then, fueled with dangerous anarchy by the CIA.

The second Memorandum, NSAM 57, reinforced the effects of the first *Memorandum*, and followed it up. It stated that the CIA can only act in small clandestine operations. Here is the text: [172]

Any large paramilitary operation wholly or partly covert which requires significant numbers of militarily trained personnel, amounts of military equipment which exceed normal CIA-controlled stocks and/or military experiences of a kind and level peculiar to the Armed Services is properly the primary responsibility of the Department of Defense with the CIA in a supporting role.

It would have been the end of that *status quo* that left the CIA free to change the world's geo-political map as it wished with coups d'états. However, it was bad luck that at the same time JFK met with an unexpected, naive and also misguided refusal. His plan, very well-orchestrated, foresaw the placing of his brother, RFK, at the head of the Central Intelligence Agency. But Bob Kennedy declined, objecting to the public embarrassment that their relationship as brothers would have caused, probably even much greater than the one, already great enough, which had been created by the nomination of RFK in the role of Attorney General. This refusal obliged JFK to fall back on another choice: John McCone. [173]

---

[172] Department of State, *Foreign Relations of the United States, 1961–1963, Volume VIII, National Security Policy*

[173] Schlesinger, *A Thousand Days; John F. Kennedy In The White House*; Schlesinger, *Robert Kennedy and his times*

Perhaps because it was a rushed job, almost *in extremis*, the choice of McCone was in no way a brilliant move, but a blinding error for which JFK paid a great price. In fact, McCone's character was so vile that when, some years later, he became the director of ITT, an industry which, for its high importance due to its work in telecommunications, had always been very close to the CIA, he did not hesitate in helping the fall of the legitimate President of Chile, Salvador Allende, this way causing the rise of the neo-nazi dictatorship of Augusto Pinochet Ugarte. Among the documents which show it, there is a secret communication, dated September 12, 1970, between Kissinger and Nixon, in which the then Secretary of State informed the US President of a phone call with McCone the previous evening, in which he favored an 'iron fist' against Allende. [174] But how vile McCone was, is nevertheless revealed by his aforementioned involvement in the anti-JFK front along with Sindona, Andreotti, William Harvey and Renzo Rocca. [175] It means, in short, that JFK was tricked twice: for his resorting to McCone to replace Allen Dulles, and also for the fact that Allen Dulles became one of the components of the Warren Commission. This last mockery was underscored by JFK's nephew, RFK Jr., who wrote in American Values:

Allen Dulles told a young writer in 1965, "That little Kennedy, he thought he was a god." LBJ would later appoint Dulles to the Warren Commission investigating Jack's assassination, a curious choice at a time when some Americans, including my father, suspected the CIA's involvement in JFK's murder.

But the devastating power of this mockery is made clearer than ever before in light of the links between Allen Dulles and CMC. Let's see them.

---

[174] The National Security Archive, *Transcript of a Telephone Conversation Between President Nixon and the President's Assistant for National Security Affairs Kissinger*, September 12, 1970, 12:32 p.m.
[175] Roberto Faenza, *Il Malaffare*

THE LINK BETWEEN ALLEN DULLES AND THE CMC

It has already been mentioned how the *Centro Mondiale Commerciale* papers which I finally retrieved record the presence of both the banker Hans Seligman and the banking institute he owned, which was known by the full name of Hans Seligman-Schurch & Co., with headquarters in Basel. Well, this bank, during WWII, was mentioned inside two very special lists: the British Statutory List and the American Proclaimed List. [176]

What was it about? I will leave it to an excellent authority on the matter to explain: The National Archive. This is their elucidation: [177]

The British Statutory List was very similar to the American Proclaimed List, in that it published the names of persons and firms in areas outside of enemy control who had in some way rendered significant aid to the enemy war machine, and that those listed were proscribed from trading with the British Empire

In other words, Hans Seligman-Schurch & Co. was guilty of collaborating with the Nazis. This fact raised the alarm in 1957 for the US Consulate in Basel, which issued various extremely worried dispatches. The most relevant ones were from January and February of that year. Let's start with the last one. [178] It explains how in Switzerland preparations were in full swing concerning Permindex, which, as we know, was the parent company of CMC. And these preparations not only unnerved the Consulate due to the connections between Permindex and this very disreputable bank, but also because

---

[176] *Foreign service dispatch from American Consulate, Basel to the Department of State in Washington. Proposed permanent international industrial exhibition (PERMINDEX). February 1, 1957*

[177] www.archives.gov/research/holocaust/finding-aid/civilian/rg-353.html#13

[178] *Foreign service dispatch from American Consulate, Basel to the Department of State in Washington. Proposed permanent international industrial exhibition (PERMINDEX). February 1, 1957*

one of the figures within this company had created, during WWII, a veritable traffic of Jews, whom he removed from Nazi persecution only if they would pay him. And who was this figure? It was the previously mentioned George Mandel alias Giorgio Mantello, who was involved in the CMC speculation at Capocotta. On Seligman Bank and the CMC, the Consulate in Basel had already expressed itself negatively in its January document, attached to a dispatch entitled MEMORANDUM CONCERNING THE PERMINDEX PROJECT. It was written directly from the pen of the Consul John A. Lehrs, a diplomat with a career beginning in 1918. But here, the Consulate also refers to another bank. We read:

The Consulate has been informed in strict confidence by a reliable source that Mr. Nagy's "American financial group", which is supposed to supply the project with the necessary funds, is headed by what has been referred to as the "Schroder Bank in New York", meaning undoubtedly either the J. HENRY SCHRODER BANKING CORPORATION or the SCHRODER TRUST COMPANY, both of 57 Broadway, New York

And yet, despite the stark facts, the State Department on June 4, 1958 issued a directive which was unexpectedly disturbing. Given its importance, it is quoted here in full:

DEPARTMENT OF STATE INSTRUCTION

N° CA- 10596   June 4, 1958

SUBJECT: Permanent International Industrial Exhibit (Permindex)

To: Amembassy ROME
    Amconsul BASEL

FROM COMMERCE

Dr. Ferenc Nagy, the ex-Prime Minister of the last non-communist government of Hungary, called on the Acting Director of the Office of Trade Promotion, Bureau of Foreign Commerce, on May 19, 1958, to report on the latest developments with respect to Permindex, which now plans to open in Rome, instead of Basel, as originally planned. Previously, Dr. Nagy had called on several officials of the Department of Commerce at different times to seek support for Permindex. He was informed at that time that the Department is interested in all ventures of the type of Permindex which seek to promote world commerce, and that appropriate assistance in the form of publicity in Foreign Commerce Weekly would be given to the trade mart if and when it should become an accomplished entity.

Dr. Nagy is expected to call on the Embassy at Rome to acquaint it with Permindex and possibly to request assistance in furthering the aims of the enterprise. The offer made earlier to Dr. Nagy is still good and the Embassy is requested to keep Commerce informed of progress in this endeavor. Should the Permindex become a going concern a report on its ownership and conditions under which American firms might participate should be submitted.

A copy of confidential despatch N°. 55 of April 9, 1958, from the Consulate at Basel giving the history of Permindex in Switzerland is attached for the background of the Embassy.

DULLES

Enclosure: Confidential D-55, 9/4/58 (For Rome Only)

Who was the Dulles who had signed at the end of the document? He was John Foster Dulles, then Eisenhower's Secretary of State, but above all brother of *Allen* Dulles. Well, what explains Foster Dulles's reaction? The answer lies in various things which the Consulate ignored. One is in another document, declassified only very recently. This time, it is a 1959 paper, and it was issued by the IOD (International Organizations Division), the CIA branch occupied in psychological warfare both at home and abroad, and, at that time, in infiltrating countries in the Soviet bloc. Here are its first two points: [179]

---

[179] CIA. HSCA Segregated CIA Collection, (microfilm - reel 17: Ruiz-Webster), *Memorandum: Subject - Trace results on persons connected with Centro Mondiale Commerciale (World Trade Center)*. NARA Record Number: 104-10181-10114

1. Dr. Ferenc Nagy, former prime minister of Hungary, presently resident in the United States, and a covert associate of IOD is President of Permindex, a Swiss corporation with principal offices in Rome and representatives in various parts of the world. The World Trade Center, in which Nagy is also interested is associated with Permindex. Brochures describing these organizations are attached.

2. Nagy has asked a representative of IOD if CIA would be interested in:

   a) Placing an American businessman on the Board of Permindex.
   b) Placing a CIA agent on the staff of Permindex.
   c) Purchasing some shares in Permindex through the above representative on the Board in order to have a voice in the management of it. (Nagy emphasized that the firm is well financed and that this is not a pitch for funds).

It is well worth stopping here and decrypting every single line. We should begin by understanding what the role of a "covert associate" is. As provided by the Clandestine Services Instruction No. 10-5 and by the Clandestine Services Instruction - Field No. 10-5, whenever the CIA utilizes coverts associates, it gives them a security clearance, a contract and a salary. So, clearly, the covert associate is a figure very similar if not identical to that of an agent of the Central Intelligence Agency. Yet the contract for "covert associates" specifies that these can neither define themselves nor be defined by others as employees of the Central Intelligence Agency. This oddity has, obviously, an important explanation: the covert associate is a figure to be used as a smokescreen on very secret and sensitive missions whenever the CIA needs to deny its own involvement. This is precisely because a covert associate is not, by definition, a CIA agent. The covert associate is therefore a very potent figure. Evidence of this strength is that it was Cord Mayer, the head of the IOD, the CIA official who signed the Memorandum and invested all his energy in pouring his heart out in favor of Nagy.

In other words, what the Consulate in Basel had not understood was, first of all, that it was dealing with a company headed by a figure who was well-placed in the very top level of the US power structure. And in fact, Nagy, at point 2 on the document, was *himself* the one who suggested to the CIA that they should have a US business man in the CMC-Permindex. This, if we connect it specifically with point 2b, sounds wholly like a proposal to have in the CMC a US businessman connected to the CIA. This is really interesting in light of the fact that at that moment the CMC-Permindex *already* had in its Board of Directors a US businessman, who was Clay Shaw, appointed on July 24, 1958. So, all in all, this could all be seen as an invitation by Nagy to make Shaw the CIA's point of reference and control inside the CMC. The exact same Clay Shaw, that is, incriminated by Garrison for the deadly shooting in Dallas. But there were two other essential things that the diligent diplomatic officials in Basel ignored. The first was the action, behind the Seligman Bank, of a law office called Sullivan and Cromwell. [180] This law office was the one that Allen Dulles and John Foster himself had worked for. [181] What a scam! But this information should be tied to another blunt fact: Allen Dulles, during the era in which he was head of the CIA, possessed, through the other CMC-financing bank, the Schroder of New York (a.k.a. Schrobanco, as we know), an expenses fund which he operated directly. It was a disproportionate, colossal deposit, considering that it contained the sum of fifty million dollars of the time. [182] It was an amount the bank was absolutely keen to maintain, due to the conspicuous advantages which the institute had obtained precisely from the coups organized by the CIA. [183]

---

[180] Mellen, *A farewell to Justice*
[181] THE NEW YORK TIMES: Stephen Kinzer, *When a C.I.A. Director had scores of affairs*, November 10, 2012
[182] DiEugenio, *Destiny betrayed*
[183] DiEugenio, *Destiny betrayed*

We are referring, for example, to the one in 1953 in Iran. In fact, the J. Henry Schroder Banking Corporation was the financer of the Anglo-Iranian Oil, the petroleum company that exploited the Iranian crude oilfields. [184] An emblematic example of what I mean is Frank Tiarks, who, besides his role as director of AIOC, was nonetheless an essential figure in both the J. Henry Schroder as well as the Schrobanco, [185] so much so that: [186]

In 1938, Frank C. Tiarks (1874-1952), Managing Director of J. Henry Schroder & Co. in London and a director of the Bank of England in 1912-1946, acted as Hitler's financial representative in Great Britain. [...] Tiarks became particularly involved in the business affairs of three private banks in Cologne, notably J. H. Stein, the family firm of Baron Bruno [von Schroder]'s wife, Deichmann & Co., and Sal. Oppenheim & Cie.
The interests of Schroders in Germany were managed predominantly by the merchant firm, Schroder Gebruder, in Hamburg, and its affiliated bank in Cologne, the J.H. Stein & Co. in which SS-Oberfuhrer Baron Kurt von Schroder was a partner. Kurt von Schroder was also Hitler's representative to the Bank for International Settlements and a director of International Telephone & Telegraph (I.T.T.) subsidiaries in Germany.

The Bank for International Settlements, or BIS for short, which we will discuss again shortly, is a sort of central Bank of Banks, with ample immunity benefits in its transactions. [187] As well as its deep connections with Hitler, we should add the links existing between Tiarks and the British Union of Fascists. [188] This English party nurtured the objective of a military alliance between the United Kingdom and Nazi Germany, as well as a military pact between the United Kingdom and the Anglo-German Fellowship. [189] This last

---

[184] Kinzer, *The Brothers*
[185] LeBor, *Tower of Basel*
[186] Martin Erdmann, *Building the Kingdom of God on Earth*
[187] LeBor, *Tower of Basel*
[188] Lightbody, *The Second World War: Ambitions to Nemesis*
[189] Forbes, *Doing business with the Nazis*; Clive Fletcher, *The Duke of Windsor's last secrets*

was an association headed by Joachim von Ribbentrop, the Foreign Minister of the III Reich. All of these facts together make tragically predictable what happened to Mohammad Mossadegh when, after becoming the Iranian Prime Minister, he nationalized the local *black gold* resources – Dulles promptly removed him.

But the shadow of Schrobanco also looms over the 1954 coup in Guatemala, which involved the CIA agent Hunt. Yes, the same Hunt later connected to the murder of JFK, as we well know. Well, to be more precise, in Guatemala the Schrobanco was joined by United Fruit, the US multinational which had much to do with what can reasonably be defined as an actual colonialization of Central and South America by the United States. The point is that also United Fruit was linked – yet again! – to the Dulles brothers. [190]

[United Fruit] was a prized Sullivan & Cromwell client. Both Foster and Allen did legal work for United Fruit, and both reportedly held substantial blocks of United Fruit stock. Sullivan & Cromwell also represented the two affiliated companies through which United Fruit secured its power over Guatemala: American & Foreign Power Company, which owned Empresa Eléctrica de Guatemala, producer of most of Guatemala's electricity, and International Railways of Central America, which owned its rail network. The J. Henry Schroder Banking Corporation, another longtime Sullivan & Cromwell client, served as financial agent for all three companies.

This conspiracy between United Fruit, the Dulles and a bank linked to the CMC, offers an important observation: New Orleans, the city where the plot that killed JFK was set up and planned, is one of the places in the United States where the structures of United Fruit were the most developed, branched out and established. That is just the start. In fact, to all of this we should add the entrance of Allen Dulles in 1937 on the Board of Directors of Schrobanco, as documented by the historian Adam LeBor. We read: [191]

---

[190] Kinzer, *The Brothers*
[191] LeBor, *Tower of Basel*

Kurt Freiherr von Schröder […] was one of the most powerful and influential bankers in Nazi Germany, a scion of the dynasty whose empire included J. Henry Schröder in London and Schrobanco in New York, whose board Allen Dulles joined in 1937. Sociable, cosmopolitan, and well-traveled, von Schröder was known as a reliable, international financier, part of the new global elite who were equally at home in the gentlemen's clubs of London or the dining rooms of Wall Street. The German banker was especially close to Frank Tiarks, the director of the Bank of England who was a partner in J. Henry Schroder bank in London. Tiarks had set up Schrobanco in New York, recruiting Gates McGarrah to its board. Between 1923 and 1939 Kurt von Schröder regularly traveled to London and frequently met Tiarks. The two men had "many business talks together," von Schröder later testified. While in London, von Schröder arranged loans for the Flick industrial concerns, whose head, Friedrich Flick, was pouring money into the Nazi party. The loans, like most of Kurt von Schröder's arrangements, went through his relative Baron Bruno von Schröder, the head of the London branch of J. Henry Schröder banks. Kurt von Schröder also did business with several other major British banks, including Guinness Mahon, Kleinwort, and Lloyds, all on behalf of J. H. Stein, the influential private bank in Cologne where he was a partner.

Hjalmar Schacht personally appointed von Schröder to the BIS board.

To recap: we can see both Allen Dulles's removal from the CIA by Kennedy, in order to avoid the repetition of coups like the ones in Guatemala and Iran, as well as the changes described in the NSAM 55 and 57 Memoranda, as very valid motives for the CMC to go after JFK. Moreover, the direct connection between Schacht and von Schröder outlined in the passage by LeBor above, was another excellent explanation for the disturbing reply given by Foster Dulles to the alarm on the CMC by the Consulate of Basel. In fact, as we will shortly see, Gutierez Spadafora, Schacht's father-in-law was a member of the CMC. And let's add to this that in 1940 the President of BIS became Thomas McKittrick, who was a member as well of its BOD since 1931. [192] Well, who was he? LeBor explains: [193]

---

[192] LeBor, *Tower of Basel*
[193] LeBor, *Tower of Basel*

McKittrick had long been a good friend of Allen Dulles, whom he had first met when Dulles was working at the American Legation in Bern and Dulles assisted him with a visa matter. McKittrick well understood that Sullivan and Cromwell offered an entrée in the covert world where politics and diplomacy met transnational finance. In September 1930 McKittrick wrote to a colleague, "We are seriously considering throwing some legal work to Sullivan and Cromwell in order to get benefit of Dulles services in many directions." McKittrick also arranged short-term loans to the German government. McKittrick's German loans were watched appreciatively at the BIS and Sullivan and Cromwell. In October, Gates McGarrah, the BIS president, wrote to John Foster Dulles expressing how glad he was that the "Lee Higginson [German] credit got itself through.

This means that under the roof of the Schrobanco, financer of the CMC, there were, shoulder to shoulder, Allen Dulles and Frank Tiarks. Under the roof of the BIS, shoulder to shoulder, were Kurt von Schröder and Hjalmar Schacht. The latter had personally selected von Schröder to be on the Board of Directors of the BIS. So, it is really time to explore who these two figures were.

KURT VON SCHRÖDER AND NAZISM

In the historian Joachim Fest's famous biography of Hitler, this passage appears:

As president of the Cologne Herrenklub, [Kurt von] Schroder had extensive connections throughout heavy industry in the Rhineland. He had actively supported Hitler on various occasions, had sketched plans for Nazi economic policies, and in November, 1932, had signed the petition drawn up by Hjalmar Schacht blatantly backing Hitler's claims to power.

Herrenklub was a definition for the elite aristocratic circle in favor of Nazism. To be complete, Kurt von Schröder did not only sign the petition, but because of his close relations with the cream of Germany's most right-wing industrialists, he had convinced many of them to support Schacht's call. Not only that, but in January 1933 von Schröder's home at Cologne had been the place of a fundamental meeting organized to establish Nazism. Kurt's guests included Hitler in person; Franz von Papen, ex-Chancellor; Rudolf Hess, top Nazi gerarch; Heirich Himmler, head of the SS; and Wilhelm Keppler, coordinator of funds given by German industrialists who supported Nazism. During this meeting, Hitler specifically planned that Farben would produce synthetic oil and rubber to avoid the need to import these products in their natural forms from abroad. [194] The encounter was undeniable since a Berlin newspaper, the *Tägliche Rundschau*, published a picture showing the invited guests stepping over the threshold of Kurt von Schröder's mansion. Kurt von Schröder would always maintain an extremely privileged rapport with Himmler, and, thanks to the baron's zeal, Heirich Himmler would secretly receive substantial secret funds. How? Through an account in Himmler's name, concealed as the single letter S. [195] The account had been opened in the aforementioned J. H. Stein Bank owned by Kurt von Schröder. And Stein Bank, as we saw, was connected with Tiarks. Kurt von Schröder's accomplice in this action was Hermann Schmitz. It is significant that he was the CEO of Farben, and also a Board member of the BIS. [196]

HJALMAR SCHACHT AND NAZISM

As for Hjalmar Schacht, one of his most appropriate portraits was without doubt provided by William Shirer, who in his rightly acclaimed The Rise and Fall of the Third Reich, writes:

It is obvious, then, that in his final drive for power Hitler had considerable financial backing from a fairly large chunk of the German business world. [...] One of the most enthusiastic of them at this time [...] was Dr. Schacht, who

---

[194] LeBor, *Tower of Basel*
[195] LeBor, *Tower of Basel*
[196] LeBor, *Tower of Basel*

resigned his presidency of the Reichsbank in 1930 because of his opposition to the Young Plan, met Goering in that year and Hitler in 1931 and for the next two years devoted all of his considerable abilities to bringing the Fuehrer closer to his banker and industrialist friends and ever closer to the great goal of the Chancellor's seat.

On Schacht, Shirer also cites, quite rightly, the contents of certain letters to Hitler. Here is one: [197]

"I have no doubt that the present development of things can only lead to your becoming Chancellor . . . Your movement is carried internally by so strong a truth and necessity that victory cannot elude you long . . . No matter where my work may take me in the near future, even if someday you should see me imprisoned in a fortress, you can always count on me as your loyal supporter." One of the two letters from which these words are taken was signed: "With a vigorous 'Heil.'"

The relationship between Hitler e Schacht is eloquently shown through these other facts: [198]

In the secret Defense Law of May 21, 1935, he [Hitler] appointed Schacht Plenipotentiary-General for War Economy, ordering him to "begin his work already in peacetime" and giving him the authority to "direct the economic preparations for war." The inimitable Dr. Schacht had not waited until the spring of 1935 to start building up the German economy for war. On September 30, 1934, less than two months after he had become Minister of Economics, he submitted a report to the Fuehrer entitled "Report on the State of Work for War-Economic Mobilization as of September 30, 1934," in which he proudly stressed that his ministry "has been charged with the economic preparation for war." On May 3, 1935, four weeks before he was made Plenipotentiary for War Economy, Schacht submitted a personal Memorandum to Hitler which began with the statement that "the accomplishment of the armament program with speed and in quantity is *the* [italics his] problem of German politics; everything else therefore should be subordinate to this purpose . . . " Schacht explained to Hitler that since "armament had to be camouflaged completely until March 16, 1935 [when

---

[197] Shirer, *The rise and fall of the Third Reich*
[198] Shirer, *The rise and fall of the Third Reich*

Hitler announced conscription for an army of thirty-six divisions], it was necessary to use the printing press" to finance the first stages. He also pointed out with some glee that the funds confiscated from the enemies of the State (mostly Jews) and others taken from blocked foreign accounts had helped pay for Hitler's guns. "Thus," he cracked, "our armaments are partially financed with the credits of our political enemies."

THE OLD FRIENDSHIP BETWEEN SCHACHT AND THE DULLES

But there is another important connection to be outlined, and it is the one between Schacht and the Dulles brothers. To understand how huge this was, let's begin with the words of the previously mentioned historian Adam LeBor, who writes: [199]

[There's a] John Foster Dulles's central role in channeling funds from the United States to Nazi Germany in the 1930s. Indeed, his friendship with Hjalmar Schacht, the Reichsbank president and Hitler's minister of economics, was crucial to the rebuilding of the German economy.

LeBor recalls them in a review of another acclaimed work by his peer, Kinser. The book is entitled The Brothers, and contains this passage: [200]

In mid-1931 a consortium of American banks, eager to safeguard their investments in Germany, persuaded the German government to accept a loan of nearly $500 million to prevent default. Foster was their agent. His ties to the German government tightened after Hitler took power at the beginning of 1933 and appointed Foster's old friend Hjalmar Schacht as minister of economics.
Allen had introduced the two men a decade earlier, when he was a diplomat in Berlin and Foster passed through regularly on Sullivan & Cromwell business. They were immediately drawn to each other. Schacht spoke fluent English and understood the United States well. Like Dulles, he projected an air of brisk authority. He was tall, gaunt, and always erect, with close-cropped hair and high, tight collars.

---

[199] THE NEW YORK TIMES: Adam LeBor, *Overt and Covert*, November 8, 2013
[200] Kinzer, *The Brothers*

Both men had considered entering the clergy before turning their powerful minds toward more remunerative pursuits. Each admired the culture that had produced the other. Both believed that a resurgent Germany would stand against Bolshevism. Mobilizing American capital to finance its rise was their common interest.

In effect, Schacht's parents had married in the United States, living there for five years, and Hjalmar had nearly met the same fate as his brother William who, because of his birth in the USA, had become a US citizen. [201] But to return to Kinzer:

Working with Schacht, Foster helped the National Socialist state find rich sources of financing in the United States for its public agencies, banks, and industries. The two men shaped complex restructurings of German loan obligations at several "debt conferences" in Berlin—conferences that were officially among bankers, but were in fact closely guided by the German and American governments—and came up with new formulas that made it easier for the Germans to borrow money from American banks. Sullivan & Cromwell floated the first American bonds issued by the giant German steelmaker and arms manufacturer Krupp A.G., extended I.G. Farben's global reach, and fought successfully to block Canada's effort to restrict the export of steel to German arms makers. According to one history, the firm "represented several provincial governments, some large industrial combines, a number of big American companies with interests in the Reich, and some rich individuals." By another account it "thrived on its cartels and collusion with the new Nazi regime." The columnist Drew Pearson gleefully listed the German clients of Sullivan & Cromwell who had contributed money to the Nazis, and described Foster as chief agent for "the banking circles that rescued Adolf Hitler from the financial depths and set up his Nazi party as a going concern."

It was the wrong point of view which pushed Foster Dulles to also support America First, a movement which believed in US neutrality towards Hitler and which, if it had prevailed, would almost certainly have caused a Nazi triumph in the War. In the light of all this, it was very clear in what great danger the Dulles were at the opening of the Nuremburg Trials after the end of WW2. There was

---

[201] Frédéric Clavert, *Hjalmar Schacht, financier et diplomate (1930-1950)*

a risk that their unsavory activities could have exploded around them like a bomb. But the danger was quickly and expertly defused by the brothers. In fact, if it was true that the head of the US delegation at the International Court was Robert Jackson, a man of rare integrity, unfortunately his deputy was the intimate right-hand man of Allen Dulles, William Donovan. It was the Donovan we have met many times before, starting with his recruitment of Luigi Crocco, the scientist brother of the CMC member Alfredo Crocco.

HANS BERND GISEVIUS

As soon as Schacht arrived to be examined at the High Court, it set off a volley of telegrams between the State Department and the US diplomatic representatives in Berlin and Zurich. The aim of the telegrams was to ensure the deliberate arrival in the Bavarian town of Hans Bernd Gisevius. [202] He was a Nazi soldier who became, after WWII, one of the OSS agents most strongly connected with the activities of Allen Dulles in Switzerland. Their friendship was even close enough to share, quite peaceably, a lover, Mary Bancroft. [203] Having been catapulted – literally – into the Court, Hans Bernd Gisevius provided Schacht with a staged, bogus defense which portrayed the famous German banker as a long-time opposer of Hitler. This was a clash with reality of such massive proportions that it elicited a strong response from Robert Jackson. In a tough cross-examination – and the word tough here is used euphemistically – Jackson demanded that Schacht enlighten the court as to who, according to the banker, might actually be considered Nazi criminals. Unable to avoid answering the very awkward question, Schacht finally babbled

---

[202] LeBor, *Tower of Basel*
[203] THE NEW YORK TIMES: Robert McG. Thomas Jr., *Mary Bancroft Dead at 93; U.S. Spy in World War II*, January 19, 1997; THE INDEPENDENT: Godfrey Hodgson Monday, *Obituary: Mary Bancroft*, February 17, 1997

some names – Hitler, Goering, Bormann, von Ribbentrop, Heydrich. With admirable quickness, Jackson then picked up a pile of photographs and placed them in front of Schacht. In all the pictures the banker appeared repeatedly next to each of these men. Schacht, concluded Jackson with finality, *must* be condemned. But, as is well-known, honest skill is no match for an opponent with a rigged hand. Gisevius's cheating hand is really self-evident when we know what he absolutely avoided revealing in Nuremberg. That is, first of all, his key role in the secret German attempt to convince the United States to ignite a Third World War on the still smoking ashes of WWII. And a Third World War that would have been to feature Nazi and US troops marching side by side together against the USSR. [204] Note that this plan was backed by Himmler. It means the same Himmler covertly subsidized thanks to the complicity between Kurt von Schröder and Hermann Schmitz. It was the Schmitz, as we know, simultaneously CEO of Farben and Board member of the BIS. And guess by whom this Himmler's endorsement to Gisevius was supported? But by Allen Dulles, of course. In fact, this is what Christopher Simpson in his book The Splendid Blonde Beast wrote about:

During the winter of 1942, the SS sent German socialite and businessman Max Egon von Hohenlohe to meet Dulles in Bern and feel out the possibilities for a U.S.-German rapprochement. Dulles and von Hohenlohe had known one another for almost of twenty years, and their reunion in Switzerland was congenial. Dulles went to considerable lengths to convince the SS that he favored a rapid settlement with Germany. He told von Hohenlohe that he was "fed up with listening all the time to outdated politicians, emigres and prejudiced Jews," according to captured German reports on the meeting now in U.S. archives. Germany would inevitably become a "factor of order and progress" in Europe following a settlement of the present conflict, Dulles indicated, and should be permitted to keep Austria and several other territories that Hitler had already claimed. Dulles "did not seem to attach much importance to the Czech question," the meeting notes continued. "He favored enlargement of Poland eastwards [into the USSR] and the

---

[204] Peter Hoffmann, *History of the German Resistance, 1933-1945*

maintenance both of Romania and a strong Hungary as a cordon sanitaire against Bolshevism and Pan Slavism. ... He regarded a greater Germany, federated on American lines and allied to a Danube confederation, as the best guarantee for the orderly reconstruction of Central and Eastern Europe."

Dulles told the SS envoy that "due to the inflamed state of public opinion in the Anglo-Saxon countries," the U.S. government would not accept Hitler as a postwar chief of state. But it might be willing to negotiate with a National Socialist Germany led by another powerful Nazi, such as SS chief Himmler. In a second meeting, Dulles advised Hohenlohe that the SS should "act more skillfully on the Jewish Question" to avoid "causing a big stir." There would be no war crimes trials for Nazis, obviously, with Himmler as head of state.

[...]

Recently opened OSS archives make clear that Dulles favorably reported to Washington on an offer [of a separate peace] from Hohenlohe at the same time Hohenlohe was reporting to the SS that the initiative came from Dulles. On the U.S. side, the OSS cables show that Dulles lobbied on Hohenlohe's behalf, ensuring that the proposal would be considered directly by President Roosevelt, and continued to pursue contacts with Hohenlohe and other SS representatives for the remainder of 1943. While Dulles was not blind to the possibilities of using the negotiations simply as a means of sowing dissension in the SS, all of the available telegrams indicate that he saw Hohenlohe's proposal as a realistic and desirable basis for U.S. strategy in Europe. On the German side, captured SS records and the memoirs of Walter Schellenberg (a Himmler protégé and the chief of the SS foreign intelligence service) each indicate that the proposal was seriously considered by Himmler himself.

[...]

The fact that Dulles and the OSS went to considerable lengths to keep the negotiations secret from Stalin also suggests that the agency wanted to keep the door open to serious negotiations with Nazi Germany for a separate peace, if only as a contingency for the future. If all that Dulles and the OSS had desired was a psychological ploy to disrupt Nazi unity, then why not inform the USSR of what was up. and in so doing avoid any risk of damaging the strategic U.S.-Soviet alliance? The OSS and the NKVD shared secrets concerning other highly sensitive intelligence operations, but there is no evidence in the available records that the OSS attempted to do so in this case. That it did not seems most consistent with the conclusion that OSS leaders believed that separate peace negotiations could not be completely ruled out.

Yes, it all fits. And the pieces of the puzzle continue to interlock if we see who else Gisevius forged a strong relationship with: Gero von

Gaevernitz. [205] Gero von Gaevernitz who had already been Allen Dulles's right-hand man for years. Their connection included the creation, through Dulles, of a puppet enterprise in New York, first named *Schildge Rumohr*, and then *Transmares*. This puppet enterprise was in reality needed to cover activities financed by Schroder Bank and which required secrecy. [206] It was, as we have seen, an impressive preview of the CMC itself.

And the pieces of the puzzle continue to fit also when we know that Mary Bancroft, the previously mentioned lover of both Dulles and Gisevius, was an excellent friend of Ruth Forbes Paine Young, who was none other than the mother of Michael Paine. Michael was the husband of Ruth Hyde Paine, a regular social frequenter of Oswald and his wife, Marina Oswald. Ruth Paine would contribute decisively in creating the legend of Oswald as a lone-nut killer. [207] This legend was so useful in diverting the investigation into Kennedy's death away from the hypothesis of a plot, which it actually was. Besides, Ruth Paine's father, William Avery Hyde, was part of the Agency for International Development created by the CIA to cover some of its clandestine activities [208] while Sylvia Hyde Hoke, Ruth's sister, was actually *officially* a CIA agent, as was proven by documents declassified years later. [209] As for Michael Paine, he was a heavyweight in Bell Helicopter, [210] a US war industry which reaped enormous profits from the Vietnam War. The War which JFK, as

---

[205] Peter Hoffmann, *History of the German Resistance, 1933-1945*; Richard Breitman, *U.S. Intelligence and the Nazis*

[206] Glen Yeadon, *The Nazi Hydra in America*; Burton Hersh, *The old boys. The American Elite and the origins of the CIA*

[207] Evica, *A certain arrogance*; Gibson, *The Kennedy assassination cover-up*; Douglass, *JFK and the unspeakable*; THE ASSASSINATION CHRONICLES: Graf, Bartholomew, *The gun that didn't smoke*, Spring 1997

[208] Weberman, *Coup d'Etat in America*; see also Douglass, *JFK and the unspeakable*

[209] CIA, HSCA segregated CIA collection, *Security file on Sylvia Hyde Hoke,* July 30, 1971. NARA Record Number: 1993.07.24.08:39:37:560310

[210] Douglass, *JFK and the unspeakable*

expressed very clearly in documents, was in the process of stopping, had he not been killed. The point is that Ruth Paine's shadow appeared also during Jim Garrison's investigation on the assassination of JFK. In fact, when Marina Oswald was asked whether she still frequented Ruth Paine, she said: [211]

No, I like her and appreciate what she did. [But] I was advised by Secret Service not to be connected with her, seems like she was .. not connected .. she was sympathizing with the CIA. She wrote letters over there and they told me for my own reputation, to stay away.
[...]
They didn't say anything personal about her, but they said its better for me to stay away from her for a while, it seemed like she was sympathizing with CIA.
[...]
Seems like she had friends over there and it would be bad for me if people find out connection between me and Ruth and CIA.

At that point, she was blatantly asked:

In other words, you were left with the distinct impression that she was in some way connected with the CIA?

Her answer was "Yes".
Not only: as written by the essayist Glen Yadon, there was another less edifying aspect to the relationship between Gisevius and Allen Dulles. This one: [212]

Declassified files show that Slovenian bishop, Gregory Rozman, was trying to arrange the transfer of huge quantities of Nazi-controlled gold and Western currency that had been discreetly secreted in Swiss banks during the war. The bishop had been sent to Berne with the aid of Dulles' friends within the intelligence service. For a few months, the Allies were successful in preventing Rozman from

---

[211] Garrison's investigation on JFK Assassination, *Orleans Parish Grand Jury testimony of Marina Oswald Porter,* February 8, 1968
[212] Yeadon, *The Nazi Hydra in America*

102

receiving the funds. Then suddenly, Rozman had the funds for his Nazi friends residing in Argentina. Dulles had fixed it. This action may be only the tip of the iceberg. In 1945, the U.S. Treasury Department accused Dulles of laundering the funds from the Nazi Bank of Hungary to Switzerland. Similar charges were made against Dulles' agent Hans Bernd Gisevius, who had worked as an OSS agent while serving at the Reichsbank. The State Department quickly took over the case from the Treasury, after which the investigation was silenced and quickly dropped.

Gregorij Rožman, bishop of Ljubljana during WWII, was at the top of the pro-Nazi Slovenian Clerical Party, and an avid supporter of ferocious civilian persecutions committed by Erwin Rösener, the head of the *Schutzstaffel* in Slovenia. [213] As for the involvement of the Bank of Hungary, which we mentioned previously, it should be emphasized that Hungary was the birthplace of the aforementioned Ferenc Nagy, the anti-communist politician, member of the CMC. Nagy fled to Budapest at the end of the war and later took refuge in Dallas, the scene of the fatal crime against JFK. But by coincidence Hans Gisevius also emigrated to Dallas. Anyway, his transfer to this city has such strong implications that it will be better to pursue the matter in a few pages.

THE RESCUE OF KURT VON SCHRÖDER

To recap, by now it is evident that Schacht's absolution at Nuremburg was part of the scheme to protect the Dulles' conniving with the Nazis. This takes us straight to the Schrobanco which later financed the CMC. To put it another way, getting Schacht off at the International Trials was directly functional for getting Schröder off too.

There was, however, a catch. At the end of Hjalmar Schacht's acquittal, a new element appeared concerning the complicity between the Krupp industries and Hitler. The proof was extremely serious. Krupp industries had not been ashamed to use concentration camp

[213] Aaron, Loftus, *Ratlines*

prisoners as forced labor, exploited by Krupp as no more than slaves. This new evidence had convinced the delegates of the countries forming the prosecution at Nuremburg (France, United States, Britain and the USSR) to rightly declare that it was highly appropriate, in order to prosecute Krupp, to institute a second international trial, analogous to the first one just concluded. On this matter, below is what Telford Taylor, Jackson's close collaborator, wrote: [214]

Upon my return to Nuremberg at the end of April, Mr. Justice Jackson appointed me as his representative to consult and cooperate with the other three prosecution delegations with respect to a second IMT trial, and instructed me in accordance with the communications exchanged between himself and the War Department. The representatives so appointed by the four chief prosecutors met on three occasions between 15 May and 9 July 1946. Primarily, consideration was given to the selection of defendants. All four delegates agreed that, in the interests of an expeditious trial, the number of defendants should be held to a minimum, and not exceed six to eight, including Alfried Krupp, who had already been designated as a defendant by the Committee of Chief Prosecutors in November 1945. By the time of these meetings, evidence had become available deeply implicating the principal directors of the I. G. Farben chemicals combine in slave labor and other criminal activities, and American interest in exposing the full scope of Farben activities was acute as a result of revelations by a special Senate Committee headed by Senator Harley Kjlgore. Consequently, I recommended the inclusion of at least two leading directors of I. G. Farben, suggesting Hermann Schmitz (Chairman of the "Vorstand," or Managing Board of Directors) and Georg von Schnitzler (a leading member of the "Vorstand" and chairman of its Commercial Committee). Mr. Elwyn Jones of the United Kingdom requested the inclusion of the well-known Cologne private banker, Kurt von Schroeder (at whose home Hitler and von Papen had reached the understanding which ultimately led to Hitler's designation by von Hindenburg as Chancellor), and M. Dubost of France proposed Hermann Roechling (the leading coal and steel magnate of the Saar). The representative of the Soviet, Union reserved the right to suggest one or two additional names, but never did so. Consequently, the five names agreed upon for inclusion in a second London Charter trial, should one take place, were those of Alfried Krupp, Schmitz and Schnitzler of I. G. Farben, Roechling, and Schroeder.

---

[214] Taylor, *Final Report to the Secretary of the Army on the Nuremberg War Crimes Trials under Control Council Law No. 10*

Anyway, in the end the United States preferred to build a case *by themselves* against Krupp. So, not the expected International Court, but an exclusively American one. In this trial, *coincidentally*, the name of Kurt von Schröder did not appear again amongst the defendants. And the trial concluded with a definite conviction for Alfried Krupp of 12 years and the loss of his company, but with the subsequent overturning of the woefully inadequate conviction because, after only two and a half years, Alfried Krupp received a pardon. From whom? From John McCloy, [215] a lawyer and a banker who, from September 2, 1949 to August 1, 1952, was acting as USA High Commissioner for Germany. So, he was able to use this role to grant a pardon. And a pardon so thoughtful to even annul the sanction which provided for the subtraction of Krupp's assets. [216]

The feeling that McCloy's actions were not in good faith is greatly supported by the results of another of his rescue operations. This time it was for Herta Oberheuser, freed despite being found guilty of having conducted inhuman experiments on women and even children in the concentration camps of Ravensbrück. She injected gasoline into their little bodies while they were still alive, and even removed organs without anesthesia, as they screamed in agony. [217] But a further example of McCloy's lack of sincerity emerged when he managed to liberate another convicted defendant of the Krupp case, Hermann Schmitz. Schmitz, as we have seen, was very closely connected to von Schröder and to Himmler, who was in turn connected to Gisevius, Schacht's savior at Nuremburg. Schmitz had been present in positions of command in the BIS as well as Farben.

---

[215] Jacobsen, *Operation Paperclip*; LeBor, *Tower of Basel*
[216] LOS ANGELES TIMES: Robert Sherrill, *The real McCloy*, April 19, 1992
[217] VIERTELJAHRSHEFTE FÜR ZEITGESCHICHTE: Thomas Allan Schwartz, *Die Begnadigung Deutscher Kriegsverbrecher. John J. McCloy und die Häftlinge von Landsberg*, 1990, Third issue.

Well, guess what? McCloy had been legal assistant of Farben.[218] And the Farben industry, together with Krupp, was connected through a law firm linked to both Dulles – Allen Dulles, head of the CIA, as well as Foster, his brother and Secretary of State. The legal company was Sullivan & Cromwell, of course. LeBor remembers:[219]

Sullivan & Cromwell floated bonds for Krupp A. G., the arms manufacturer, and also worked for I. G. Farben, the chemicals conglomerate that later manufactured Zyklon B, the gas used to murder millions of Jews. Of course, the Dulles brothers' law firm was hardly alone in its eagerness to do business with the Nazis — many on Wall Street and numerous American corporations, including Standard Oil and General Electric, had "interests" in Berlin.

Farben, at this juncture, had two branches, the German one and the American one. The commercial division of the American one was General Dyestuffs, headed by a US citizen, Ernest Kay Halbach. The Pearl Harbor disaster – the bombardment by the Japanese, allied to the Nazis, that almost crippled the United States – could, and should have been a good moment to finally open the eyes of Washington to the situation. And indeed, so it seemed:[220]

After Pearl Habor, the U.S. Treasury blocked Halbach's bank accounts. In June 1942 the Alien Property Custodian seized Halbach's stock in General Dyestuffs and took over the firm as an enemy corporation under the Trading with the Enemy Act. Subsequently, the Alien Property Custodian appointed a new board of directors to act as trustee for the duration of the war. These actions were reasonable and usual practice, but when we probe under the surface another and quite abnormal story emerges.

The anomaly was Louis Johnson, assigned by the US government, to head General Dyestuffs as a controlled company. The job was paid 75,000 dollars a year, of that time, and Johnson, a former

---

[218] LeBor, *Tower of Basel*
[219] THE NEW YORK TIMES: Adam LeBor, *Overt and Covert*, November 8, 2013
[220] Sutton, *Wall Street and the rise of Hitler*

Special Assistant for the Ministry of War, should in any case have known how to do his duty, but instead, he did the opposite: [221]

pressure to bear on the U.S. Treasury to unblock Halbach's blocked funds and allow Halbach to develop policies contrary to the interests of the U.S., then at war with Germany. The argument used to get Halbach's bank accounts unblocked was that Halbach was running the company and that the Government-appointed board of directors "would have been lost without Mr. Halbach's knowledge."

Not only that, but under these mounting pressures, Halbach lodged a series of legal actions against the Alien Property Custodian. And the legal firm which assisted him in this disastrous pursuit was no other than Sullivan & Cromwell linked to the Dulles. Here are the details: [222]

Leo T. Crowley, head of the Alien Property Custodian's office, had John Foster Dulles as his advisor, and John Foster Dulles was a partner in the above-mentioned Sullivan and Cromwell firm, which was acting on behalf of Halbach in its suit against the Alien Property Custodian.

These legal actions were later refuted but the sly motives for which they had been made had achieved the desired result, which was to allow Halbach, for the duration of the war, to avoid the expropriation.

In a nutshell, if the case concerning the murky dealings between Hjalmar Schacht, Allen Dulles, Kurt von Schröder (scion of those Schröders, financiers of the CMC linked to JFK's death) was never allowed to get to court, it was all due to the joint work of Dulles and McCloy. Yet another example of this deadly synergy between Dulles and McCloy in protecting Nazis had already been put to use when they had combined their forces to face another very different pair: Roosevelt's Secretary of State, Henry Morgenthau – who was also

---

[221] Sutton, *Wall Street and the rise of Hitler*
[222] Sutton, *Wall Street and the rise of Hitler*

the father of Robert M. Morgenthau, the Prosecutor we met before – and his assistant, Harry Dexter White. In September 1944, both politicians had drafted a plan ready to severely punish industrialists who had supported Hitler. McCloy, then, immediately acted to systematically boycott this plan, while on the other hand, supported the need to rearm Germany as soon as possible as an anti-Soviet force. These efforts by McCloy were rewarded with West Germany being allowed to enter the military alliance known as NATO just ten years after the fall of the Third Reich. [223]

As for Allen Dulles, he had already, by the summer of 1945, drafted a list of eight Germans who "for their ability and curriculum" he recommended to revive industrial production in West Germany. Among those listed appeared two of Hjalmar Schacht's protégées. The first was Ernst Huelse, general director of BIS, and nonetheless Schacht's right arm in the Reichsbank; the second was Karl Blessing, also a man with a significant past both with the Reichsbank and the BIS. But Blessing was also a close friend of Schacht. That's how Blessing became the head of the West German Central Bank. At the same time, thanks to Dulles's prompt alacrity, Blessing's assiduous presences (thirty-eight of them) at the so-called *Himmlerkreis* meetings, the circle of industrialists closest to Himmler, would be completely silenced. So assiduous was Blessing that he was the go-between for secret funds to Himmler through the aforementioned account, concealed behind the code-name S, at the J. H. Stein Bank of Kurt von Schröder. [224]

THE BUSH FAMILY

But in reality, though, those who profited from the cover-up of Kurt von Schröder's crimes were not only McCloy and the Dulles.

---

[223] See Adam LeBor, *Tower of Basel*
[224] Christopher Simpson, *The splendid blond beast*

There were even the Bushes twice residents in the White House. To explain how, let's turn back to Gisevius running to rescue Schacht at Nuremburg. As previously stated, after Nuremberg Gisevius emigrated to Dallas where he joined Dresser Industries. [225] Dresser was in the oil business, and its consultant was de Mohrenschildt. [226] This means the very same de Mohrenschildt who inexplicably associated with Oswald; the same de Mohrenschildt nonetheless supervisor to Herbert Itkin, the CIA agent not only linked to anti-Castro activities but also to one of the protagonists in Borghese's coup: Pier Talenti. The connection with the Bushes? On the Dresser Board of Directors, was also Prescott Bush, [227] father of George H. Bush. In other words, inside Dresser there was also the father of an individual who became head of the CIA and then President of the United States. The Presidency also passed on to George W. Bush, son of George Herbert, and therefore, grandson of Prescott. The point is Prescott Bush had many strong contacts with Kurt von Schröder. Kurt von Schröder, in fact, was co-administrator of the famous German foundries Thyssen, alongside Johann Groeninger, partner of Prescott Bush in the Union Banking Corporation of New York. UBC was similarly linked to Thyssen and, even more, to a bank that had been really generous to the Nazis, the *Voor Handel en Scheepvaart* of Rotterdam. Von Schröder, moreover, was both vice-president and administrator of the Hamburg-America Line, an international delivery company which had covertly supplied weapons to Hitler. [228] As the essayist Yeadon writes: [229]

---

[225] Phillips, *American Dynasty*; THE ASSASSINATION CHRONICLES: Graf, Bartholomew, *The gun that didn't smoke*, Spring 1997

[226] CIA, Russ Holmes work file: *Col. Lawrence Orlov: educational and professional record*, NARA Record Number: 104-10431-10034

[227] Tarpley, Chaitkin, *George Bush. The unauthorized biography*; Yeadon, *The Nazi Hydra in America*; Kelley, *The Family. The real story of the Bush dynasty*

[228] Yeadon, *The Nazi Hydra in America*

[229] Yeadon, *The Nazi Hydra in America*

[Prescott Bush] was instrumental in setting up a deal to take over Hamburg-America Line, a Nazi front company used for espionage. Prescott Bush hired Allen Dulles to hide his assets invested in Germany from authorities. In 1942 Prescott Bush was charged with running Nazi front groups and those assets were seized

Finally, there existed a dense and long correspondence between Bloomfield, founder of Permindex-CMC, and George H. Bush. This correspondence is kept in the previously mentioned documents submitted by Bloomfield himself, as explicitly expressed in his will, to the Library and Archives Canada. However, they are still inaccessible due to the earlier cited veto by Bloomsfield's widow. The importance of having access to this correspondence is certainly exposed by, first of all, a document by the FBI. [230] It shows George H. Bush as being part of the CIA in 1963, and the one whom Hoover contacted immediately after Kennedy's death. This means a role in the CIA *since 1963* that was so important that it pushed *the head* of the FBI to contact George H. Bush in the aftermath of the killing. George H. Bush whose father had links with the von Schröder scion of the financers of the CMC connected with the plot to kill JFK, as I just explained. But it means also that there is no oddity at all in George H. Bush's choice, from January 30, 1976, to January 20, 1977, as head of the CIA. In fact, that position, for obvious reasons, usually goes to someone who already has a long career in the Agency, and the FBI document is proof that George H. Bush actually *had* that long career. Especially so considering another document, discovered in 2006: an internal CIA Memorandum of November 29, 1975, entitled Messrs. George Bush and Thomas J. Divine. [231] The context;

---

[230] HSCA, FBI investigative files on assassination of JFK, *Memorandum from Hoover, Anti-Castro activities*, November 29, 1963. NARA, Agency File Number: 62-109060-1396. Record Number: 124-10264-10221 - Records Series: Ho Agency File Number: 62-2115-6

[231] CIA, Deputy Director for Plans Files, Memorandum for Deputy Director of Operations, *Messrs. George Bush and Thomas J. Divine*, November 29, 1975. NARA Record Number: 104-10310-10271

the qualifications of the memo's writer as chief of secret commercial operations; the fact that his identity is still censored and identified only by a number [03], the presence of the phrase "secret commercial operations in Europe", all these tell us that this document was alluding to something also the CMC was part of: CIA operations *disguised as* mercantile activity. Really disturbing. Even more so, since the code-name for these operations was WUBRINY. Yes, this was the name of the field operation in 1963 in Haiti, as we know. To seal it all, if everyone living at the time remembers where they were and what they were doing when Kennedy was killed, George H. Bush is the exception.

WORLD BROTHERHOOD

Having resolved this latest, very disruptive piece of the puzzle, we should move on to another. Namely, an association with a double identity like the CMC, and called World Brotherhood; officially dedicated to propagating world peace, but in reality, doing the opposite. The first reason for examining it is because it had both Allen Dulles and John McCloy in it. Yes, once again the couple also part of the Warren Commission supposedly created to seek the truth about the murder of JFK.

For sure, a first clear clue on World Brotherhood's real intent emerges from a letter to Dulles on April 2, 1958 recommending Dulles' support to World Brotherhood. It defined the organization to the CIA chief as the way to «tremendously help the efforts to which you are dedicated». [232] The true meaning of the message comes from knowing who the members of its General Assembly were. [233] Aside from McCloy and Dulles, among them there was

---

[232] CIA, General Records, *Letter from James N. Rosenberg to Allen W. Dulles*, April 2, 1958. Document Number (FOIA)/ESDN (CREST): CIA-RDP80B01676R003800180046-4
[233] World Brotherhood Organization 1949 - 1956; Allen W, Dulles Papers; Public Policy Papers, Department of Rare Books and Special Collections, Princeton University Library

nonetheless Thomas McKittrick, who was, as we know, also the president of the Bank for International Settlements. But World Brotherhood also included Alfredo Pizzoni, last seen as the go-between for Dulles to finance *Pace e Libertà*, the anti-Marxist organization headed by Edgardo Sogno and CMC member Pièche. But in World Brotherhood there was also Vittorio Valletta, another generous subscriber to Sogno's cause, as well as that of the head of Italian Intelligence: Renzo Rocca. You may recall Rocca was linked to the CMC member Alfredo Crocco, whose brother, Luigi Crocco, had been personally recruited by Donovan as a scientist useful to the USA. The fact is that Donovan also was part of World Brotherhood. This was the same Donovan who had intervened to save Schacht from being convicted at Nuremberg, but also the same Donovan associate of Gigliotti, the CIA agent and freemason purposely sent to Italy in 1960 to seal a plot with the local Freemasons against JFK. The masonic pact against JFK was concurrent with the letter Gigliotti sent to Nixon, Kennedy's rival for the White House, to ensure him that the Freemasons would have done anything to help the Republican win the election. It is surely worth remembering that Allen Dulles and Hjalmar Schacht were Freemasons too. But it is nonetheless worth knowing that there is another letter, which makes very clear that a strong sympathizer of World Brotherhood was actually Nixon himself. [234] As much as knowing the existence of another letter, [235] in which we find the name of one of the *founders* of World Brotherhood. It was sent to Allen Dulles by Carlos Rómulo, then Foreign Minister of the Philippines, and the founder revealed was James Zellerbach, the US Ambassador. It means the same Zellerbach was also co-signatory to the pact between US Freemasons and Italian

[234] Central Intelligence Agency, General Records, *Letter from Vice President Richard M. Nixon to Mr. Everett Clinchy*, August 17, 1959. Document Number (FOIA)/ESDN (CREST): CIA-RDP80R01731R000200070031-3

[235] Rómulo, Carlos P. 1957-1966; Allen W. Dulles Papers; Public Policy Papers, Department of Rare Books and Special Collections, Princeton University Library

Freemasons, which had a secret clause stating they would stop JFK at all costs. As confirmation, this connection between Zellerbach and World Brotherhood was echoed in an article dated March 17, 1959 in the Italian daily *La Stampa*, which includes the following:[236]

The Ambassador of the United States to the Italian government, Mr. James D. Zellerbach, has concluded his stay in Piedmont by participating yesterday in Turin at a meeting of "World Brotherhood". This organization – born in 1950 in Paris, home of UNESCO – aspires to the collaboration between peoples through educational methods and scientific research.

The piece in *La Stampa* relates that Zellerbach was given a special honor which makes the whole thing unequivocally clear. It reads:

The ambassador was awarded a medal for "exceptional merit" by "World Brotherhood". […] The President of Fiat, professor Valletta, in his quality as founder member and member of the presidential committee of "World Brotherhood" welcomed Mr. Zellerback […] "In World Brotherhood," continued the orator, "you are one of the most deserving American founders. […]

CMC AND ISRAEL

But Zellerbach, aside from that, was also a key member of the international Jewish community. This fact should be joined to another: it was World Brotherhood, really, who was steeped in Israel. In fact, its founder was Everett Clinchy, who forged it expressly as the spare rib of another of his creations: The National Conference of Christians and Jews. These elements allow space for one of the most shocking aspects of the plot against JFK. It was that the same CMC was born with a very deep connection with Israeli Intelligence. We already know the diatribe about Permindex between US diplomacy in Basel and the State Department, arising because a key figure of

---

[236] LA STAMPA: *Consegnata all'ambasciatore Zellerbach la medaglia della "Fraternità Mondiale"*, March 17, 1959

this company was the shady Georges Mandel. The dispute was concluded with a disturbing letter from Foster Dulles which, outside the mask of protocol, can be translated as follows: *"The CMC has my personal support, shut up and leave them to work".*

Well, there is another very important American document, a Memorandum of 1959, and it is totally dedicated to Mandel. [237] After returning many times to witness accounts of his immorality and dishonesty, this Memorandum, at Point 5, makes a very detailed but also formidable revelation: witnesses identified Georges Mandel *alias* Giorgio Mantello, as belonging to the Israeli spy network. To prop up this affirmation, the document emphasizes that Mandel, in 1951, was employed in the *Banque pour le Commerce Suisse-Amérique Centrale* in Geneva, "which supplied cover employment for IIS [Israeli Intelligence Services] agents". The annotation to Point 5 is a knock-out of the kind where the referee counts to 10 just as a formality: within the said bank, Mandel was the right arm of another Bank member. This latter was someone whose activities for the Israeli espionage were significant and well known to US Intelligence.

But that a very strong link between Israel and CMC existed is indubitably at its best demonstrated directly by my own exclusive papers. In fact, they show that on the Board of Directors of CMC was Gershon Peres. He was there from 1967. This is an enormous revelation because we are talking about the brother of Shimon Peres, President of the State of Israel from 2007 to 2014. During his presidency, there was an attack with white phosphorus against Palestine, which caused the death of hundreds of children. But Shimon Peres is also linked to another presence inside the CMC: namely, Alberto Forte. In the 1970s he was Managing Director of the *Banque Belgo-Centrade*. This bank was a subsidiary of the Swiss-Israel Trade

---

[237] CIA. HSCA Segregated CIA Collection, (microfilm - reel 17: Ruiz-Webster), *Memorandum: Subject - Trace results on persons connected with Centro Mondiale Commerciale (World Trade Center)*. NARA Record Number: 104-10181-10114

Bank in Geneva. The Swiss-Israel Trade Bank was created by a very important Jew, Yehuda Assia, who by his own admission, had put up half the necessary capital, while the other half had been sent directly by the government of Israel. And behind this bank – the story was reconstructed by the Israeli newspaper *Haaretz* – was Mossad. Not only that, but Yehuda Assia had taken the role of collector of necessary funds for the creation of the Negev Nuclear Research Center of Dimona, thanks to which today Israel possesses atomic missiles. And Assia's role was conferred on him *precisely* by Shimon Peres. [238] The Dimona Center drew very strong objections from JFK, who did not desire Israel to have atomic weapons. In fact, he rightly believed them to be an immense obstacle to a project close to his heart: a world ban on thermo-nuclear bombs. [239]

But there is more. The *Banque Belgo-Centrade S.A.*, which was created before JFK's death, was officially connected to another one in New York: Chase Manhattan Bank, of David Rockefeller. Chase Manhattan Bank that, in turn, was connected to the shady alliance between the Vatican and P2 signed in the shadow of the high prelate Paul Marcinkus. [240] Finally, the *Banque Belgo-Centrade* continued to be a subsidiary of the Swiss-Israel Trade Bank even when the SITB changed its name to *Banque pour le Commerce Continental*. Under this transformed label, it was behind the money, sponsored by the CIA, given to the Chilean truck drivers' union to paralyze the country with strikes during the last weeks of Salvador Allende's presidency. [241]

---

[238] HAARETZ, Ofer Aderet, *Yehuda Assia banker to the Mossad, dies at 99*, September 3, 2016; WEIZMANN INSTITUTE OF SCIENCE, *Interview with Yehuda Assia*, May 1, 1997

[239] See Seymour Hersh, *The Samson Option*; Mearsheimer, Walt, *Israel Lobby and US Foreign Policy*; Mattson, *Stealing the atom bomb*; Avner Cohen, *Israel and the bomb*

[240] THE NEW YORK TIMES, Paul Lewis, Italy's mysterious, deepening bank scandal, July 28, 1982; Ingo Walter, *The secret money market*; Barrese, Caprara, *L'Anonima DC*; Gianni Flamini, *Il Partito del golpe – 1971*; Caroline Pigozzi, *Le Vatican indiscret*

[241] LIBRES AMÉRIQUE: Samuel Jordan, *Quarante apres la chute d'Allende: Quand la Suisse fêtait le putsch*

The strike was successful in the intent for which it had been artificially created: that is, to bring about Allende's destruction and the creation of Pinochet's Nazi dictatorship. And in fact, next to Alberto Forte, on the Board of the *Banque Belgo-Centrade* we find the Chilean extreme right-winger Arturo Klein. [242] What is so shocking is that both Klein and *Banque pour le Commerce Continental* were mentioned in a US top secret classified document now kept in the Reagan Library, which reveals that the bank as well as Klein were involved in a plot to kill President Jimmy Carter. Exactly. And the motive was precisely Carter's nuclear policy which, like JFK's, was not favorable to Israel. [243] So close is the connection between CMC and Israel that it even involves the place where Oswald was accused of having fired from on that November 22. The owner of the building and, consequently, the one who rented it to the Texas School Books Depository, the company that operated from there and employed Lee Oswald, was David Harold Byrd. This ultra-conservative magnate was a friend to JFK's sworn enemies, including General Curtis LeMay [244] and the oil magnate H. L. Hunt. [245] He is the very same H. L. Hunt about whom I have already demonstrated his connection to the shooting of JFK. Byrd, like Hunt, was rich with oil properties, but also – coincidentally – uranium. [246]

However, the controlling interest of his empire, Byrd Oil, including Byrd Uranium Corporation, since 1956 had passed into

---

[242] See *The bankers' almanac* 1970s issues

[243] Ronald Reagan Library, *United States Senate. Committee on Foreign Relations. Report concerning activities of certain Foreign Intelligence Agencies in the United States submitted to the Subcommittee on International Operations*, January 18, 1979

[244] Byrd, *I'm an endangered species*

[245] John Hughes-Wilson, *JFK. An American Coup d'Etat*; William Reymond, *JFK. Le dernier temoin*

[246] THE UNIVERSITY OF TEXAS, DEPARTMENT OF GEOLOGY, *Newsletter n. 5*, July, 1956; see also TIMES-NEWS, *Buys interest*, June 29, 1955; THE SANDUSKY REGISTER: Phyllis Battelle, *Assignment America*, March 15, 1956

the hands of A. M. Abernethy. [247] At this passage, A. M. Abernethy was elected president, while Byrd himself had remained as Board Chairman, and the company name remained Byrd Oil. [248] But the point is that Abernethy, in turn, was under control of another very important Jew, Arie Ben-Tovim. [249] This latter, was the Israeli Consul in Montreal between 1949-50, and then Consul in New York between 1951-52. [250] But the most relevant fact is another: Arie Ben-Tovim was also in the CMC. A fact that is even more interesting considering what was revealed by Sol Estes, a whistle-blower belonging to a privileged circle of friends making up the cream of Dallas's most powerful. Estes declared D. H. Byrd was involved in the plot against JFK. [251] But the existence and consistence of links between CMC and Israel are also shown by the presence, on the CMC Board of Directors, of Dov Biegun. Already a member of the British Intelligence during WWII, Dov Biegun was the general secretary of the National Committee for Labor Israel. This was an institution whose aim is to forge an unbreakable relationship between Israel and the United States. An effort that the NCLI was able to grant encouraging, for example, the acquisition in the US of Israeli bonds: a move indubitably crucial to the constitution and strengthening of the Israeli state. Besides, in the NCLI, there were preponderant conservative trade unions radically in favor of the expansion of the Vietnam War. As I explained before, it was the

---

[247] QUIXOTIC JOUST, Linda Minor, *Other Uranium explorers in Texas in the 1950's*, June 11, 2011
[248] THE KERVILLE TIMES, *Group buys Harold Byrd Oil interests*, April 30, 1956; see DEL RIO NEWS HERALD: *Buy control*, April 29, 1956
[249] See THE LETHBRIDGE HERALD, *Markets*, May 9, 1953; QUIXOTIC JOUST, Linda Minor, *Did D. Harold Byrd sell out to Israelis?*, August 15, 2011
[250] Zachary Kay, *Diplomacy of prudence. Canada and Israel, 1948-1958*; JEWISH TELE-GRAPHIC AGENCY, *Ben-Tovim assumes position of Israel Consul in New York. Served in Canada*, February 8, 1951; *Israel appoints new Consul for Los Angeles. New Israeli Consul arrives in Montreal*, March 7, 1951; see also various issues, from 1949 to 1950, of THE CANADIAN JEWISH REVIEW
[251] William Reymond, *JFK. Le dernier temoin*

opposite of what JFK had been trying to do if he had not been killed. Not to mention the accusation that Philip Agee, a former CIA agent, made against the NCLI of conniving with the Central Intelligence Agency. [252] Facts that have much to do with what we see today: the NCLI connections to unions blamed for attempting to ignite right-wing coup d'états in Venezuela. [253] Biegun, moreover, was part of the Jewish National Fund, a group which even now takes away Palestinian land through legal loopholes, turning them into Israeli property. But apart from Vietnam and the previously mentioned opposition of JFK to Israel's nuclear armament, the leaders of the Jewish state saw Kennedy as the enemy also because of his fair policy towards the Arab world. This policy was demonstrated by JFK's support for the petroleum oil politics of Enrico Mattei and the end of colonialism.

As further proof, it is enough to look at a document on the failed plot to kill JFK during the President's tour of Chicago. The shooting was practically a copy of the one in Dallas just twenty days later, including the choice to divert the investigation into the truth with a scapegoat, but it failed only because of a last-minute tour call off. In this document there is a declaration made by one of the people involved, Homer S. Echevarria, a right-wing extremist. It reads: [254]

Reference is made to the office Memorandum to the chief from acting SAIC Maurice G. Martineau, Chicago, dated November 26, 1963, under file No. 2-1-611.0. [...]
For the information of all offices concerned, 2-1-266 advised on November 26, 1963, that he had heard that one Tom Mosley allegedly had been attempting to negotiate a sale of machine guns to one Homer S. Echevarria and that Echevarria allegedly made a comment the day before the assassination of President John F.

---

[252] Canfield, Weberman, *Coup d'Etat in America*
[253] LABOR FOR PALESTINE, Bob Mattingly, *U.S. Unions bankroll Israeli aggression*, August 10, 2002
[254] Warren Commission, Commission Document 87 - Secret Service report of 08 Jan 1964 re: Oswald

Kennedy that: "we now have plenty of money – our new backers are Jews" and would close the arms deal "as soon as 'we' [or 'they'] take care of Kennedy...."

But the links between CMC and Israel include the CMC member Alfredo Crocco. As we know, Crocco had a brother, Luigi, recruited by William Donovan, the head of the OSS, the US spy agency precursor to the CIA. Luigi Crocco was a long-time friend and collaborator of the scientist Theodore von Kármán. You may remember I already outlined how von Kàrmàn was one of the fathers of the RAND Corporation, a fanatically anti-communist think-tank working in osmosis with the Pentagon, and responsible for the most senseless US escalations during the Cold War. And I also described von Kàrmàn's role as president of AGARD, the special branch of NATO with the objective of coordinating scientists with the most contributions to the Western war machine. AGARD whose Italian representative was Giuseppe Gabrielli, who was none other than the brother-in-law of Alfredo and Luigi Crocco. What I will now add is that von Kármán was also, and above all, an extremely prominent Jew, who was moreover President of the Department of Aeronautical Engineering at the Israel Institute of Technology in Haifa, another place at the center of the Israeli nuclear ballistic development. Development which – I repeat – JFK opposed. This matter has an astonishing parallel precisely through the previously mentioned H. L. Byrd. Thanks to Johnson's support, Byrd would be the winner, through his Ling-Temco-Vought, of the tender for the construction of the A-7 Corsair II, an aircraft heavily used – once again – in the Vietnam War. [255]

But deeply connected to the Israeli élite was also Louis Bloomfield, the founder of Permindex, the head company of the CMC. Bloomfield's papers, as I have already narrated, were left by him to

[255] John Hughes-Wilson, *JFK. An American Coup d'Etat*; Dale Scott, *The Dallas conspiracy*; Tim Fleming, *JFK and the end of America*. Specifically, on Ling-Temco-Vought: Robert Sobel, *The rise and fall of the conglomerate kings*

the Library and Archives Canada. The archive was first explored by the researcher Maurice Phillips. As I showed in the first pages of this work, one of the documents discovered there by Philips was a letter by Bloomfield dated April 1, 1959. What I have so far omitted for reasons of consistency of the book, is that this letter was written to Abraham Friedman, member of the Israel Continental Oil Company. In this letter, Bloomfield says he wishes to meet the famous Jewish banker Edmund Rothschild to discuss with him the CMC operation at Capocotta. [256] This operation – you will remember – was in reality a mask devised by the CMC itself to buy those who held power in Italy. Indeed, those involved included the fascist General De Lorenzo as well as Admiral Giuseppe Pighini, a former high-ranking military official under fascism and then a high-ranking military figure in NATO. It was the same Pighini who received millions of dollars from Sindona in order to establish a fascist government in Italy, during the 1970s, with military support, as we know. [257] Finally, no less deep was the connection with Israel of the CMC member Roberto Ascarelli, a major representative of the Italian Jewish community, but, at the same time, owner of the law firm in central Rome, Piazza di Spagna 72/A. The place that, on the one hand was connected to CMC, and on the other, to the first important steps of P2. P2 headed by the fascist Gelli thanks not only to Ascarelli but also to a second CMC member: Virgilio Gaito.

But this intrigue between Israel and fascism was a distorted idea which unfortunately took root in the birth of Israel itself. When the UN resolution of 1947 decided that a part of Palestine, Jewish holy land, was to be given to the Jews, this did not exactly please the

---

[256] From *The Permindex papers II, The unknown Permindex story: Canadian attorneys, Venezuelan corporation and French Rothschild*, published by Phillips on his blog on May 16, 2010.
[257] ITALIAN DOCUMENT: *Commissione parlamentare d'inchiesta sul caso Sindona e sulle responsabilità politiche e amministrative ad esso eventualmente connesse. Relazione di minoranza dell'On. Giuseppe D'Alema e altri*

Egyptians, who interfered and, in military terms, became a thorn in the side of the Jewish state. In order to block and defeat the Egyptian threat, the irreparable happened: Israel did not hesitate to call on Borghese's X^a *MAS*, and in particular the fascists Nino Buttazzoni, Geo Calderoni, and Fiorenzo Capriotti. Imagine, X^a *MAS* rushing to train Jewish soldiers. This training was decisive for Israel's success in the Negev War which ended, thanks to fascist help, with a heavy Egyptian defeat. [258] But not only that: Buttazzoni could count on a strong ally, Angleton. No surprise: it was the continuation of the alliance already established between Borghese and Angleton that I already described. And Angleton it was who also established, and continually protected, a steel pact over the years between the CIA and Mossad, the Israeli Intelligence Agency. [259] Mossad that, for operations against Egypt, did not hesitate to recruit an Austrian ex-nazi official and pupil of Adolf Hitler. This was Otto Skorzeny, who, just like von Schröder and Schacht, was able to escape the judicial consequences of his war crimes. In his case, through a spectacular escape plan in July 1948, in which, as declared by Skorzeny himself, US Intelligence was accomplice to. An alliance, this between Skorzeny and Israel, which had risen despite the fact that, once he had reached safety in Spain, he became a focal point for global neo-nazism. [260] At that time, Skorzeny met Ilse von Finkenstein, who he married in 1954. And who was her uncle? He was Schacht. So, Schacht and Skorzeny were related. But there is more: in Spain, they also became accomplices in money trafficking; this too linked to neo-nazism. Yes. In fact, as Martin A. Lee writes: [261]

---

[258] See Eric Salerno, *Mossad base Italia*

[259] Ian Black, Benny Morris, *Mossad*; Eric Salerno, *Mossad base Italia*; Holzman, *James Jesus Angleton, the CIA, and the craft of Counterintelligence*

[260] Peter Levenda, *The Hitler Legacy*

[261] Martin A. Lee, *The Beast reawakens*

Treated like a celebrity, Skorzeny got lots of help from the Franco regime, which previously had close ties to Nazi Germany. Franco also provided a safe haven for Nazi financial assets that were shifted to neutral countries as the war drew to a conclusion. These hidden Nazi funds, according to a U.S. Treasury Department probe, were secretly used to acquire controlling interest in 750 business enterprises spread across different continents (including 112 Spanish firms). Hjalmar Schacht played a key role in orchestrating the transfer of large sums through a complex web of camouflaged front companies and bank accounts. Fearing that Nazi survivors would utilize the hidden wealth for nefarious purposes, U.S. investigators tried to follow the money trail but were frustrated by Schacht's intricate financial maneuvers.

Skorzeny that, no coincidence, takes us back to the CMC member Pièche. Let's see how.

GIUSEPPE PIÈCHE AND THE STRATEGY OF TENSION

In a metaphor in which the truth about the neo-fascist bomb which exploded at the end of the 1960s in the Italian city of Milan was inside a closed room, the key to get in would be a memo by the SID, espionage agency of that country. A memo of December 16, 1969, and whose contents point to a line of secret command behind the explosion. A line made up of some really interesting characters, the first of whom was Yves Guérin-Sérac, founder and head of the *Aginter Press*, a press agency which, exactly like the CMC, was not what it pretended to be, but instead a facility, a station supported and protected by the CIA, and whose goal was the so-called Non-orthodox War against communism. The other names in this line were: Robert Leroy, a Nazi sympathizer who was Guérin-Sérac's right-hand man; Mario Merlino, a fascist infiltrated among anarchists in order to deflect the investigations into the massacre by falsely blaming the Marxists. Finally, the document indicates the name of Stefano delle Chiaie, head of the Italian neo-fascist organization *Avanguardia Nazionale* (National Vanguard).

This memo was kept secret as long as possible, reason why the magistrates only obtained it in March 1973. This is a clear evidence of its importance. An importance that was strongly insisted on by Guido Salvini, the judge who more than anyone worked to search for the solution to the mystery of *Piazza Fontana* (Fontana Square), the name by which the bombing in Milan is commonly known since it was at the branch of the *Banca Nazionale dell'Agricoltura* (National Agriculture Bank) there that it occurred. The validity of this memo was substantiated by Salvini emphasizing how the details it contained were absolutely exact: the directions to the building in Paris where Leroy lived; that a time bomb device was the one utilized; that Merlino, thanks to their common holiday destination, knew the director of the financial institution which was the scene of the crime. That said, the point is that the Leroy cited in that Memo was an associate of Pièche. In fact, writings by the Frenchman appear in the Italian magazine *Vivere*, while another Italian publication, called *Il reporter politico economico*, actually *employed* Leroy. They were both periodicals under Pièche's command. [262] Not only that but at the start of the Greek dictatorship of the colonels, Pièche organized a trip to Greece so that a select group of Italian young neofascists could receive the necessary training to develop the Strategy of Tension in Italy. One of those boys, was actually Merlino. [263]

What is crucial to add is that, here too, there is something that traces back to the intermingling between Israel and the CMC's neofascism, and it is the fact that the *Aginter Press* was born of a marriage between the OAS and the so-called Gehlen Organization, the

[262] ITALIAN DOCUMENT: Atti inviati il 23 Luglio 1996 al Giudice Guido Salvini dal RAGGRUPPAMENTO OPERATIVO SPECIALE CARABINIERI Reparto Eversione. Nr.509/62 di prot. "P". OGGETTO: Procedimento penale contro Rognoni Giancarlo ed altri. Annotazione sulle attività di guerra psicologica e non ortodossa, (*psychological and low density warfare*) compiute in Italia tra il 1969 e il 1974 attraverso l'*"AGINTER PRESSE"*; Calvi, Laurant, *Piazza Fontana*
[263] De Lutiis, *Storia dei servizi segreti in Italia*

spy network of West Germany, as I already explained, headed at that time by the Nazi Gehlen, and also known as BND. Leroy, in fact, was both a member of the BND and the OAS, which instead stands for *Organisation armée secrète*. The OAS gathered together all those French people disappointed in the decision of President Charles de Gaulle to open up concessions for Algerian independence. Algerian independence that was also encouraged by JFK. Well, if we go to the Acts of that meeting in 1965 at the Hotel *Parco dei Principi* in Rome which set down the canons for how the Strategy of Tension would be conducted in Italy, it is possible to read the report submitted by Enrico de Boccard, which contains this passage:

It has also been shown, referring to France, that it is possible to put an end to, in terms of revolutionary war, the long-standing and sterile argument – even in France, as in Italy continually and artificially kept up by the communists – between fascism and anti-fascism. In the ranks of the OAS, fighting together in the same battle, we can find men from the most diverse and contrasting past experiences. We have seen, in fact, together in the lines of the OAS, ex-Resistance fighters and survivors of the German camps of Buchenwald or Mauthausen, and ex-collaborators, followers of Marshal Petain, members of the Vichy militia or fighters on the Russian front in the ranks of the Waffen SS.

But the wretched mix between Israel and neo-fascism nonetheless leads us to when Leroy, during WWII, was an instructor at the Sabotage school (Section VI) commanded by none other than the same Skorzeny [264] who, as we already said, would enter Mossad. News even more disturbing knowing that two witnesses – Adriano Monti [265] and Enzo Generali [266] – had declared that Skorzeny participated in the Borghese coup. Yes. Besides, a document exists in

---

[264] Calvi, Laurant, *Piazza Fontana*
[265] Monti, *Il Golpe Borghese*
[266] ITALIAN DOCUMENT: Commissione parlamentare d'inchiesta sulle Stragi – Doc. XXIII n.64, Vol. I Tomo II

the Archives of the Italian Polizia di Prevenzione [267] (Prevention Police). It was discovered by the historian Aldo Giannuli and kindly given to me by the *Associazione Casa della Memoria* (House of Memories Association) by Manlio Milani, to whom I am greatly indebted. This document concerns the *Unione Mediterranea Anti-comunista* (Mediterranean Anti-communist Fellowship), an organization founded in 1961 exactly by the OAS. Inside UMA, were Italian neo-fascists side by side with members of Portuguese and Spanish fascism totally supported by the dictatorships of both countries and a number of whom were "neo-Nazi elements headed by Skorzeny". The headquarters of UMA – says the document – coincides with the living quarters of Enzo Generali. Not only that but the same archive contains another really relevant document. It is the summary of statements by a Freemason dated June 19, 1971, and whose characteristics make its finder, who is once again Giannuli, aware of it being the surviving copy of an original which was destroyed purposely. Thanks to some details in it, Giannuli says, and I concur, that this Freemason is very probably a member of P2. The very same P2 which, as we know, is for many reasons undistinguishable from the CMC. In any case, here is what this Freemason states: [268]

We don't like this government [...] and we can't go on like this. The government keep on making Bolshevik laws, like the ones on housing or health reform. We are in the hands of dishonest and incompetent people who, whether they know it or not, will end up putting Italy into the hands of communism. We don't like it and neither do our American friends, for obvious reasons, and neither do our friends in Israel,

---

[267] ITALIAN DOCUMENT: Procura della Repubblica di Brescia, RELAZIONE N. 50 bis del 01.09.2006 del dott. Aldo Giannuli. Seguito documentazione J.V. BORGHESE depositata il 02.10.2006. *Borghese-Bensi*
[268] ITALIAN DOCUMENT: Procura Della Repubblica Di Brescia. Relazione di Consulenza. Procedimento penale n. 91/97 mod. 21. Provvedimento di Nomina di Consulente Tecnico e Conferimento Incarico dell'11 novembre 2003, Ex Art. 359 C.P.P. al Dott. Aldo Sabino Giannuli

who are worried about the possible repercussions that a change in the balance of forces in the Mediterranean area could have on the Arab-Israeli conflict.

And, further on:

In the first place we can count on money, on many of our friends who have key positions in Italian public life, on the support of most of the armed forces and in particular, the SID, the Carabinieri, the Finance Police, the Air Force and parts of the Navy, the special police, especially the Traffic Police, Port Police, Forest Police and on some other operative branches of the Police. The support of our friends in the United States and Israel will be decisive.

THE OAS AND THE KILLING OF JFK

But the loudest revelation has yet to come, and it is that following the above facts we will arrive at what will show us the OAS involvement in the killing of JFK. In fact, let us take another document, this time made by a special branch of the Italian *Carabinieri*. [269] It identifies the two probable handlers of Guérin-Sérac's recruitment in the CIA. The first was Philippe de Vosjoli, a very particular member of French Intelligence. His particularity resides in his transformation into a close associate with an important OAS leader, Jacques Soustelle. In fact, they both felt betrayed by de Gaulle's need to concede independence to Algeria. But for the same reason, de Vosjoli also had become close to three CIA agents of extraordinary power: James Angleton, [270] Richard Bissell and Richard Helms. [271] The result was that all the secret information that reached his desk was, from that moment on, covertly at the disposal of the CIA. The second man indicated by the Italian document about the recruitment of

---

[269] ITALIAN DOCUMENT: Raggruppamento operativo speciale Carabinieri – Gruppo Eversione, *Annotazione sulle attività di guerra psicologica e non ortodossa,* (psychological and low density warfare) *compiute in Italia tra il 1969 e il 1974 attraverso l*"AGINTER PRESSE", July 23, 1996
[270] Tom Mangold, *Cold Warrior. James Jesus Angleton: The CIA's master spy hunter*
[271] Andrew Tully, *CIA. The inside story*

Guérin-Sérac to the CIA, was Jean René Marie Souètre, a French soldier who then became another very notable figure in the OAS. Souètre who – this same Italian document adds – is also cited in a testimony by Guido Giannettini. It means, as we already know, the same Giannettini who participated, in 1965, in that meeting at the Hotel *Parco dei Principi* in Rome where the plans for the Italian Strategy of Tension were theorized. Giannettini's testimony is really important also because his being, at the same time, an agent of the Italian espionage and a prominent member of both OAS and *Aginter Press*. [272] Let's read this passage: [273]

GUIDO GIANNETTINI, in an interview on 06-08-1993 (related with paper 169/22 of 06-09-1993) and then on record given to the Judge, explained he had met **GUERIN SERAC** in 1964 in Lisbon, and presented him to Captain **SOUETRE** of the O.A.S., in the presence of an official of the P.I.D.E. [*Polícia Internacional e de Defesa do Estado*, a Portuguese Intelligence Agency].
[…]
Capt. SOUETRE is mentioned in the report of the [Portuguese Intelligence Agency] S.D.C.I. [Serviço de Detecção e Coordenação de Informações] […] as chief of an operational squad in Angola under JACQUES DEPRET. SOUETRE's squad received information from SERAC, which in turn came from the P.I.D.E.. The aim was to assist a surprise attack by MOISE TSCHOMBE in Congo [aiming to eliminate the socialist Lumumba, who was then effectively assassinated] (the matter was narrated by DEPRET himself in the book "Coup d'Etat at Brazzaville", published in Brussels in 1976).
JACQUES DEPRET, interviewed by FREDERIC LAURENT for his book "L'Orchestre Noir", published by Stock, showed on pages 140 and 141 that SOUETRE was given by SERAC the command of mercenaries recruited by AGINTER and it was proposed (to DEPRET) that he be made Information Officer, role that he accepted. He used the pseudonym CONSTANT.

---

[272] ITALIAN DOCUMENT: Commissione parlamentare d'inchiesta sulle Stragi – Doc. XXIII n.64, Vol. I Tomo II
[273] ITALIAN DOCUMENT: Raggruppamento operativo speciale Carabinieri – Gruppo Eversione, *Annotazione sulle attività di guerra psicologica e non ortodossa,* (psychological and low density warfare) *compiute in Italia tra il 1969 e il 1974 attraverso l'*"AGINTER PRESSE", July 23, 1996

Souetre is also known as JEAN RENÉ MARIE SOUETRE, alias GRAMMONT, alias MANGIN, born 15-10-1930 in Aigues-Mortes-Les Graves, son of RENÉ and SAUNAC JEANNE. Ex Captain of Aviation Parachute Commandos right-hand man of PIERRE SERGENT, head of metropolitan O.A.S..

Well, the point is he was the very same Souètre identified in an-other document, which is a really disturbing CIA Memorandum, and that reads as follows:

Jean SOUETRE aka Michel ROUX aka Michel MERTZ – On 5 March 1964, Mr. Papich advised that the French had hit the Legal Attache in Paris and also the SDECE man had queried the Bureau in New York City concerning subject stating that he had been expelled from the U.S. at Fort Worth or Dallas 48 hours after the assassination. * He was in Fort Worth the morning of 22 November and in Dallas in the afternoon. The French believe that he was expelled to either Mexico or Can-ada. In January he received mail from a dentist named Alderson living at 5803 Bir-mingham, Houston, Texas. Subject is believed to be identical with a Captain who is a deserter from the French Army and an activist in the OAS. The French are concerned because of de Gaulle's planned visit to Mexico. They would like to know the reason for his expulsion from the U.S. and his destination. Bureau files are negative and they are checking in Texas and with INS. They would like to check our files with indications of what may be passed to the French. Mr. Papich was given a copy of CSCI-3/776,742 previously furnished the Bureau and CSDB-3/655,207 together with a photograph of Captain SOUETRE. WE/3Public; CI/SIG; CI/OPS/Evans

A CIA Memorandum that becomes even more disturbing when we know the story of another *Aginter Press* member: Jay Simon Salby. This latter was, first of all, closely linked to Guérin-Sérac as well as Delle Chiaie. He used many pseudonyms: Castor, Jay Sa-blosky, Hugh Franklyn, and my research has led me to believe that the name Jay Simon Salby was actually a pseudonym too, just as Guérin-Sérac was, since his real surname was Guillou, and just as Delle Chiaie, when he worked for *Aginter*, used the pseudonym Gio-vanni Martelli, and, last but not least, just as Souètre himself, as we have seen right now, was evidently used to do. This Selby's use of pseudonyms in such a massive way, was an inevitable consequence of his life. In fact, in his past he was an American incognito involved in the failed invasion of Cuba in 1961, so much so – according to Italian documents – that Castro in person had identified him, during a radio broadcast, as an enemy of that Caribbean Island. Not only that but the Italian neo-fascist Concutelli identified Selby as a CIA man in Madrid in the 1970s, which matches Selby also being an associate of William F. Buckley. This latter was an ultra-conservative member of the CIA [274] as well as a long-term friend of Howard Hunt who was connected, as we know, to the killing of JFK. [275] Not to mention that *Aginter* was born and proliferated in Portugal when the Ambassador of that country was George W. Anderson, an admiral who entered heavily into conflict with JFK over Cuba because, during the Missile Crisis, he intended to explicitly disobey Kennedy by exploding a Soviet ship. [276] Last but not least, a CIA document records the involvement of Skorzeny, in March 1961, in operations against Castro. [277] This is a prodigious element in the life of this Nazi who went from being Hitler's pupil to being an agent of Israel. Israel present once again in another part of Giannettini's testimony. This one:

GIANNETTINI, […] who declared his becoming the outside collaborator of the S.I.D. a consequence of his ability to deepen his relationship with the O.A.S., claimed that the Americans [anti-de Gaulle] would have had a strong interest in

---

[274] ITALIAN DOCUMENT: Tribunale di Milano, Ufficio Istruzione Sezione 20, Sentenza-ordinanza del G.I. dott. Guido Salvini nei confronti di Giancarlo Rognoni e altri; DOCUMENTO: Atti inviati il 23 Luglio 1996 al Giudice Guido Salvini dal RAGGRUPPAMENTO OPERATIVO SPECIALE CARABINIERI Reparto Eversione. Nr.509/62 di prot. "P". OGGETTO: Procedimento penale contro Rognoni Giancarlo ed altri. Annotazione sulle attività di guerra psicologica e non ortodossa, (*psychological and low density warfare*) compiute in Italia tra il 1969 e il 1974 attraverso l'*"AGINTER PRESSE"*. About Salby's identity, see also: V. Chernyavsky, *The CIA in the dock*

[275] Tad Szulc, *Compulsive spy. The strange career of E. Howard Hunt*; LOS ANGELES TIMES: William F. Buckley, *My friend E. Howard Hunt*, March 4, 2007

[276] *John F. Kennedy Library President's Office Files, Presidential Recordings Collection, Tape 120/A5*; RFK Jr., American values

[277] *CIA, Special collection, Nazi war crimes disclosure act, Document Number (FOIA)/ESDN (CREST): 519bdecd993294098d514393*, February 14, 1969

a France still entangled in Algeria because this would have taken away their efforts to achieve autonomous nuclear capacity. He added that even the Israelis were interested in the French undertaking in Algeria as an anti-Arab front.

We should take care to note that there is a strong confirmation of Giannettini's words. It comes from putting together two very precise facts. In fact, if we look into the above-mentioned Soustelle, we see that before his transformation into the sworn enemy of de Gaulle, he had been the Governor of the Algerian colony. As well, Soustelle was a total sympathizer of Israel, as emerges, e. g., in the contents of his own book *La longue marche d'Israël*, published by him in 1968. An excellent explanation of why, in the spring of 1962, he organized an important visit to Israel for Giano Accame, [278] a member of the fascist *Movimento Sociale*. Accame was at the same time a pro-Israeli [279] belonging to the *Aginter Press*. [280] The second thing to add is contained in a series of articles in the Jewish magazine *Israel*, found by the historian Claudio Moffa. [281] These articles untiringly recount the origins of the acrid hostility of Israel to Algerian independence. In fact, according to the Israelis, this independence was the stepping stone to an Algerian Muslim superpower, until then kept at bay by the French presence. The magazine insisted with alarm that this was to the detriment of the wide Israeli community resident in Algeria who – according, once again, to *Israel* – risked being exterminated by the Arabs. Claudio Moffa

---

[278] Gianni Rossi, *La destra e gli ebrei: una storia italiana*

[279] A very good way to understand Accame's ideology is a series of articles he wrote in 1962 on the fascist magazine *Il Borghese: Preparano il nuovo massacro degli ebrei*, August 23, 1962; *Il comunismo contro Israele*, August 30, 1962; *I socialisti nazionali di Gerusalemme*, September 6, 1962; *Fanfani contro Israele nel Mec*, September 20, 1962

[280] ITALIAN DOCUMENT: Commissione parlamentare d'inchiesta sulle Stragi – Doc. XXIII n.64, Vol. I Tomo II; Tassinari, *Fascisteria*

[281] Moffa, *Dalla guerra di Suez all'attentato di Bascapé: l'ombra di Israele sul 'caso Mattei'*, in AA.VV., *Enrico Mattei, il coraggio e la storia*; see also Moffa's *Il "Caso Mattei" e il Conflitto Arabo-Israeliano (1961-1962)*

explained that Israel became a firm ally of the OAS just because of this absurd fear. This is a perfect echo of Giannettini's testimony.

But Accame, we should nonetheless take care to note, was also closely connected to Tambroni, the politician linked to the masonic pact against JFK, and whose son-in-law Franco Micucci Cecchi was a CMC member. The relationship between Accame and Tambroni rose through an organization named *Centro per l'ordine civile* (Centre for Civil Order). That organization also involved Accame. [282] But to tell it well, we should return to the documents discovered by the magistrate Calia. Among these, there is one concerning clandestine dealings between Fernando Tambroni and Soustelle. [283] In fact, in 1961, Soustelle secretly promised Tambroni huge financial returns linked to Algerian petroleum oil in exchange for the equally secret Italian support for the paramilitary action which, in April of that year, the *Organisation armée secrète* actually attempted in order to block the path to independence of that African country. Tambroni had such tight links to Soustelle that he would meet him even during another event in Rome on August 12, 1961. This face-to-face was celebrated "at the main level of Via Piemonte 39, at the special office of the parliamentarian Tambroni", as the SISMI papers tell us. The papers specify:

[It was] a kind of "headquarters" for the center of Civil Order (notable organization of Tambroni's), and at the same time the editorial "kitchen" of the weekly magazine "Lo Stato" [The State], the center's official voice, and probably, also the headquarters of OAS activity in Italy (at least that of high level).

---

[282] ITALIAN DOCUMENT: Commissione parlamentare d'inchiesta sulle Stragi – Doc. XXIII n.64, Vol. I Tomo II; see also LA REPUBBLICA, Paolo Mauri, *Adelphi e i balilla dell'Opus Dei*, March 27, 2001, and Piero Vassallo, *L'eredità censurata di Gianni Baget Bozzo* (on: pierovassallo.blogspot.com)
[283] ITALIAN DOCUMENT: PROCURA DELLA REPUBBLICA PRESSO IL TRIBU-NALE DI PAVIA. Procedimento penale n. 181/94 mod. 44. Richieste del Pubblico Ministero Vincenzo Calia (ai sensi dell'art. 415 p.p.) Allegato 110

It means this all happened in the same place of the Center for Civil Order. A center which not only was headed by Tambroni, as we have read, but that, as I pre-empted, also Accame was involved with. Not only that but the SISMI papers traced by Calia tell of another presence at these secret meetings between the OAS and Tambroni. It was Giovanni Amendola. Who was he? The SISMI papers tell us: "Special assistant to the parliamentarian Tambroni, [and] his figurehead in diverse financial operations". No need to say that this Tambroni's use of a front man in dealings of that kind is indubitably an excellent clue to the actual cause and aim of Franco Micucci Cecchi's presence inside CMC. Also, because, as we have seen, the headquarters of CMC and OAS both were in the same city: Rome. And because the OAS headquarters were also the general headquarters of Tambroni's political activities. [284]

CMC AND THE ASSASSINATION OF ENRICO MATTEI

Vincenzo Calia traced and put together these documents about Tambroni during the investigations into the killing of Enrico Mattei, the most iconic president of ENI. In fact, it was thanks to Calia's eminent work that we now officially have Mattei's biographies sealed with the truthful phrase "died in the skies above Bascapè because of sabotage of his aircraft" instead of the lying words "died in the skies above Bascapè because of a plane malfunction". Calia demonstrated it was an explosion which caused the crash, on October 27, 1962, of the twin-engine plane Mattei was travelling on. What trigged the explosion was a mixture of RDX and TNT, called Compound B and detected without a shadow of a doubt in the wreckage of the aircraft by investigators of Calia.

---

[284] ITALIAN DOCUMENT: PROCURA DELLA REPUBBLICA PRESSO IL TRIBUNALE DI PAVIA. Procedimento penale n. 181/94 mod. 44. Richieste del Pubblico Ministero Vincenzo Calia (ai sensi dell'art. 415 p.p.) Allegato 110

Calia was kind enough to grant me personal access to the documents he used during his inquest, and to the interrogations he made. It was exactly reading those documents and interrogations that I discovered a mention of CMC-Permindex, and in two very notable instances. The first one, direct and cutting, is when Calia interrogated Fulvio Bellini. Bellini was heard because in a book he wrote he had alluded to Mattei's death as a result of heated tensions with Eugenio Cefis, Mattei's boss. The same Cefis, as we have seen, who met with Daddario, accomplice to the liberation of Borghese; and the same Cefis in the 1970s who financed a subversive project by Sogno, close associate of the CMC member Pièche. It means that very same Sogno's project involving the so-called *Comitati di Resistenza democratica*, the subversive group the CMC member Corrado Bonfantini was part of, as we already know. In his interrogation, Bellini explicitly evoked the CMC, defining it like so: [285]

The terminal in Italy of the group who attend to all the dirty work in world politics, including the assassination of Enrico Mattei.

Bellini confirmed this idea with another comment, in which reappears the very same Soustelle at the top of the OAS. The Soustelle linked to Tambroni. Bellini said: [286]

I think that to understand the death of Enrico MATTEI you need to follow the trail to Jacques SOUSTELLE. This man was given the job of doing Operation MATTEI with around one hundred thousand dollars from Montreal, through PERMINDEX [...].

---

[285] ITALIAN DOCUMENT: PROCURA DELLA REPUBBLICA PRESSO IL TRIBUNALE DI PAVIA. Procedimento penale n. 181/94 condotto dal Pubblico Ministero Vincenzo Calia
[286] ITALIAN DOCUMENT: PROCURA DELLA REPUBBLICA PRESSO IL TRIBUNALE DI PAVIA. Procedimento penale n. 181/94 condotto dal Pubblico Ministero Vincenzo Calia

To examine the second time CMC appears in Calia's investigation, we instead need a step by step process, paying attention to a couple of really important things in the witness account released to Calia by Pietro Zullino. Zullino was a journalist, and during his work he dealt with the death of Mattei, writing down, in the 1970s, some notes which he then delivered to Calia twenty years after. These notes echo Bellini's words. In fact, they describe frictions between Cefis and Mattei. The difference is that Zullino clarifies the *specific* reason for this conflict. It was that Cefis secretly supported a competitor of ENI, Attilio Monti, an Italian oil magnate and strong rival of Mattei. Zullino writes: [287]

1. "Cefis had (and still has) strong interests in the SAROM refineries in [the city of] Ravenna and Mediterranea in [the city of] Gaeta. These refineries are among the principal suppliers of the NATO defensive systems for southern Europe and the American Sixth Fleet. They refine and sell Esso and Shell petroleum oil. Mattei was trying to force the Mediterranean NATO to become a client of ENI. Cefis opposed this project because of his interests. The incidents between Mattei and Cefis had always been numerous. Among the most serious: Cefis had facilitated an important ENI contract to the Lenci company ([to produce] gadgets to promote Super Cortemaggiore gasoline) because he was having an affair with a certain Mrs Lenci. Mattei had found the price to pay far too high and this created a horrible argument with a certain [Adolfo] Marvelli, husband of the aforesaid Mrs. Lenci (a property belonging to ENI in the EUR area of Rome was rented by the same lady, who had installed a boutique in it).
2. "Eugenio Cefis. He had been fired by Mattei in January 1962 for 'divergences' regarding ENI's politics. In reality Mattei could not tolerate Cefis having interests in RASIOM and ESSO, which supplied Mediterranean NATO and the Sixth Fleet, especially since this was happening at the same time when he [Mattei] was spending all his energy in order to ensure that ENI became supplier of both. There were other incidents. One very serious regarded a case of favoritism towards the Lenci firm, endorsed by Cefis for strictly personal reasons. CIA Agent."

---

[287] DOCUMENTO: PROCURA DELLA REPUBBLICA PRESSO IL TRIBUNALE DI PÁVIA. Procedimento penale n. 181/94 condotto dal Pubblico Ministero Vincenzo Calia

The first element to grasp is that exactly as a Mister IBM does obviously not exist, since IBM is not a person but an acronym, there is no Mister Lenci either, since, in reality, Lenci stands for the Latin phrase *Ludus Est Nobis Constanter Industria*, meaning *Playing is our constant work*. A definition that is well suited to a company specialized in making and selling toys, as Lenci was. Lenci was founded by Enrico Scavini, an Italian, and Helen Konig, a German. The woman who was Cefis' lover was, therefore, not a non-existing Mrs. Lenci, but Anili Scavini, their daughter, and effectively the creator of gadgets for ENI, the Italian nationalized company dedicated to the extraction and selling of hydrocarbons. But Anili was also creator of religious ceramics. It may be quite a fascinating explanation for the origin of the relationship with Cefis, since he was a notably avid collector of exactly this kind of item, and in the end possessed over three hundred of them. A passion in every detail recounted in the book *Questo è Cefis* (This is Cefis), which was a source of dread for Cefis on its publication since it also reported thoroughly all Cefis' ill-doings. A book, besides, that Calia discovered to be the inspiration and source for the posthumous book *Petrolio* by the Italian writer Pasolini. News that leaves one really speechless in light of my discovery that Pasolini was persecuted under false pretenses by a CMC member, as we will soon see: Giorgio Zeppieri. Pasolini was so inspired by *Questo è Cefis* in *Petrolio* that he reproduced a large part of its content. No surprise, since at the core of *Petrolio* there is Pasolini's desire to identify the puppet masters behind the Strategy of Tension and that Pasolini had already correctly understood that Mattei's death had an instrumental role in that strategy. Something well shown by a list of facts, just like, for example, the strange and prolonged presence of Max Corvo at the *Hotel delle Palme* in Palermo just before Mattei's death. [288] Corvo, as we know, was linked to both Michele Sindona and to Gigliotti. It

---

[288] De Sanctis, *Delitto al potere*

means the very same Gigliotti thanks to whom the anti-JFK masonic pact was sealed. Moreover, Mattei was killed very close to a meeting that the industrialist should have had with John Kennedy himself. A meeting where the US president would have crowned Mattei as the tutelary, the protector, of that Center-left coalition also urged by Moro. [289] But there is more: Moro was clearly the implied subject of an astonishing secret oath prepared by Edgardo Sogno, the close associate of the CMC member Pièche. Sogno's oath was taken by the accomplices of his previously mentioned subversive project, as it was revealed by Sogno himself towards the end of his life: [290]

I pledge that after any personal undertaking which may be communicated to me, to carry out, in person and alone, in the manner and time which I am told, the capital execution of political figures of democratic parties responsible for collaborating with the enemies of democracy and the betrayal of the free institutions.

The Center-left that also Rocca, the Italian spy, and William Harvey, Kennedy-hater and CIA agent in Rome, considered an illness to stop at whatever cost. The same insane vow to destroy the possibility of a Center-left that was at that same time obsessing the CMC member Alfredo Crocco, as we know thanks to Rocca's letter. The letter behind which, as I have shown, was Harvey himself. It is that very same Harvey that Howard Hunt, another CIA agent, identified in his deathbed confession as being involved in the plot to kill John Kennedy.

That said, pay attention, since Cefis too was connected to Israel. In fact, a document exists, dated December 1961, which is a list of partners of ANIC. This is a sister company of ENI, and was at that time directed by the very same Cefis. Why is this list so important? Because there were Israeli citizens in it, and the first of them even

[289] Benito Li Vigni, *Il Caso Mattei*
[290] Sergio Flamigni, *La sfinge delle Brigate Rosse*

bears the phrase "ns. agente", which stands for "our agent". This list emerged after an internal enquiry. This enquiry's origin is well-explained, once again, by the historian Moffa. Let's read his account: [291]

In the summer of '61, an official German record on petroleum oil had revealed the existence of economic relationships between ENI and Israel. The news had caused protests in the Arab world, and some countries, united in the Arab League committee to boycott Israel, had demanded explanations from Mattei. The president of ENI rushed to deny everything with strong words: "ENI does not have relationships with Israel and does not intend to have them in any form," he wrote in a letter to the Ambassador of R.A.U. in Rome on October 12, 1961. But the rumors persisted and in December, the truth came out. The relationships with Israel did exist through ANIC controlled by Cefis.

In short, as in the Lenci situation, this is a fact that shows once more how Cefis was indeed at the center of secret dealings totally at odds with Mattei's. But in retrospect it also allows us to understand why JFK had chosen Mattei as safeguard to Moro's left-wing coalition. Both Moro and Mattei, whose politics were not pro-Israel, would have contrasted, obstructed and prevented that push towards an Israeli nuclear arsenal which Kennedy strongly feared and opposed.

The second element to grasp in Zullino's deposition to Calia is a slip of the tongue. It concerns the *Mediterranea* refinery linked to the important strategic presence of NATO in Europe. The text, as we saw, says: *Mediterranea in Gaeta*. Now, if respect for a document source is sacred, then this sacredness shines a light through all of this book. But if this light shines it is because of an even greater reason: the respect I owe to the truth. So, in honor of this more important value, I must say that no *Mediterranea* in Gaeta exists. In fact, in Attilio Monti's oil empire there was, first of all, a refinery in the city of Ravenna. It was also the refinery from which

---

[291] EURASIA, Il *"Caso Mattei" e il Conflitto Arabo-Israeliano (1961-1962)*, 2007, N° 4

Monti had begun, and it was called SAROM. There was then another, operating from 1960, and whose name was actually *Mediterranea*, but which was in a Sicilian city, Milazzo. The last one was the *Gaeta Industria Petroli*, and obviously it was *this* the one in Gaeta; but it was bought by Attilio Monti only in 1969, and it was only from 1970 that it acquired the name I just said, as before it was owned by the American millionaire Getty, and named after him *Getty Oil Italiana*. So, as Pietro Zullino was outlining the disputes between Cefis and Mattei, and Mattei died in 1962, this can only have one explanation: that in Zullino's notes from the 1970s, there was an error. When he wrote *Mediterranea,* he erroneously located it in the city of Gaeta and not in Milazzo, the right one. That said, the point is that this *Mediterranea* in Milazzo was headed by Monti, but from the start he had placed it in the hands of a very particular CMC member: Gutierez Spadafora, who was also a relative of Hjalmar Schacht, as we know. Astonishing, isn't it? As astonishing as is the revelation that Monti's empire leads us also to the already mentioned fascist bombing of December 12, 1969 in Piazza Fontana. In fact, the investigators of that massacre discovered a signed letter, written by Lando Dell'Amico, an Italian journalist who had always been close to Intelligence. The letter was to Bruno Riffeser. Riffeser was Monti's son-in-law, and co-administrator, at the same time, of Monti's empire. In that letter, written just three months before the bombing, Dell'Amico narrated about a money transfer he made. This transfer was huge, and was precisely on Monti's orders. The receiver of this money was the aforementioned neo-fascist Rauti. [292] Since Rauti was one of those suspected of having links to Piazza Fontana, the legal authorities delved immediately deeper, making certain that the letter was authentic, that the existence of a financial outlay by Monti was real at the time the letter was written, and that it was the exact sum Lando Dell'Amico said. An

---

[292] Gianni Flamini, *Il Partito del golpe, VOL. II*

outlay that Monti had no plausible explanation for. At that point, Dell'Amico, realizing that the situation could put him in serious legal trouble, in two interviews during 1974 admitted that he had actually secretly passed the money to Rauti. [293]

This admission of guilt means that there was a transfer of money which clearly carried the scent of being used for the bombing in Milan. And the money came from an industrialist, Monti, owner of a refinery directed by a CMC member, Spadafora. But Spadafora was also strongly connected to another massacre, that of Portella. The Massacre of Portella which I already mentioned as related to a top-secret operation: the successful removal of De Gasperi from office. A top-secret mission carried out, as I said, by two CMC members: Azzaretto and Sagna. But by coincidence Sagna can absolutely be considered another Trojan horse against Mattei. In fact, before arriving at CMC, Sagna was on the Board of Directors of an essential ganglion in Mattei's industries: AGIP Mineraria, the branch dedicated to searching and extracting hydrocarbons. And Sagna arrived on the AGIP board in 1955 and left in 1958. It means he joined at the same time as Umberto Ortolani, and left with Umberto Ortolani. And Ortolani, as we know, was a member of P2 and a financer of Tambroni. In other words, he was a financer of one of Soustelle's strongest allies in supporting OAS and boycotting Algerian independence. But Umberto Ortolani was also a member of *Credicomin*, Borghese's so unusual bank. Yes, for the umpteenth time, everything is connected. In view of all this, exploring this link between Portella and Spadafora is therefore a well worth the effort. And an effort, besides, which we will very soon realize, is able to take us to the root of the network enemy of JFK. Let's see how.

THE CMC MEMBER SPADAFORA'S INVOLVEMENT IN THE MOST SECRET US PLANS

---

[293] Gianni Flamini, *Il Partito del golpe*, VOL. II

Let's come back to the fact that Spadafora and Schacht, a heavy-weight of Hitler's Nazism, were related to each other by the marriage of Konstanze Schacht, daughter of Hjalmar, to Michele Spadafora, son of Gutierez. [294] This marriage, it should be added, was in line with Gutierez Spadafora' past: he had been Mussolini's vice-minister. This connection with Mussolini would normally herald a long prison sentence at the end of WWII. But, just like Schacht, Schröder and Pièche, also Spadafora got away with it. Well, to be more precise, this possibility of a long sentence seemed at one point to become concrete, since in June 1945 Spadafora did end up in jail, in *Regina Coeli*, Rome's famous penitentiary. [295] But his incarceration did not last, since it was rapidly overturned by King Umberto II di Savoia, who profited from still being on the throne. In fact, it would effectively only be on June 13, 1946 that the Savoias gave in, finally leaving for exile. It means three days after the already tardy official proclamation of the result of the June 2 consultation that made Italy a republic. And so, Umberto II freed the prominent Sicilian, putting Spadafora safely out of the way of further consequences with an arbitrary gesture from a throne from which, twenty years earlier, the Savoias had already welcomed Mussolini's tyranny. In other words, this act of abuse was completed by Umberto thanks to the last vestiges of his royal privilege, as echoed in the following document that clearly shows: [296]

Prince Spadafora, neo-fascist monarchist who collaborated in the Republic of Salò, Undersecretary of State and prisoner of Regina Coeli […] was liberated by the personal act of King Umberto.

---

[294] PAESE SERA: *I personaggi del CMC-IAHC*, March 5, 1967; see also Garrison, *On the tracks of the assassins*

[295] ITALIAN DOCUMENT: Archivio Centrale dello Stato, SIS, sezione seconda, HP, busta 169

[296] Casarrubea and Cereghino, report to Magistrate Pietro Grasso

Gutierez Spadafora's improper rescue had terrible consequences which the above document, soon after, implies:

[Spadafora] is presently on a mission in Sicily, in contact with separatist leaders and neo-fascists belonging to independent groups.

In fact, this relationship of Spadafora with neo-fascists leaders aiming to make Sicily an autonomous nation, is at the root of a tragical series of events perfectly described in a document by a spy of the Italian SIS, *Servizio informazioni e sicurezza* (Information and Security Agency). It is a sort of instant detailed report about the true facts of the massacre of May 1, 1947 on the Sicilian plain of Portella. Instant since, being dated June 25, 1947, it was written not yet two months after the massacre. Let's read its content: [297]

In the month of March, to be precise, we were notified that Duke Spadafora, chief of the Agrarian Commercial Group of the South, was in Rome and had conversations with representatives of the clandestine [fascist] Front. He offered to pay a million into the account on condition that Sicily was turned into "blood-bath". Mormini, of the Front, would have had to join the Giuliano gang in Sicily, in contact also with a part of the local mafia who would be made available for his group. The proposal was not accepted. It seemed horrible…Since then, according to our accurate, verified information, Spadafora has had direct contact with [the fascist Francesco] Martina, whom he finances directly, and who obeys to his instructions. People wanted by authorities have been admitted into the band.

I would clarify that Francesco Martina was a Mussolini supporter of the *prima ora* (first hour): that is, those who were present at the March on Rome which – as I said before – led to Mussolini's inauguration by the Savoias. Besides, the phrase used in the document to describe this 'marriage' between Martina and the future CMC member Spadafora leaves no doubt that Martina was totally

---

[297] Casarrubea, *Lupara nera*

subject to Spadafora's orders. But the document also leaves no doubt about Martina's power over Giuliano, since in another point it defined him as "the real leader of the [Giuliano] gang". So, all in all, this means that Spadafora, just before Portella, took hold of the reins of the Giuliano gang, and was giving orders on what the gang did, including of course the Portella Massacre. Indeed, confirmation of the fascist nature of the slaughter can be found in another point of the SIS spy's report, in which Mussolini's nostalgic followers are described celebrating the deaths which Giuliano was causing amongst the Marxist ranks, including other bloody acts committed by Giuliano that same June 1947. This was because the neofascists considered this barrage of violence as a prelude to the imminent return of the dictatorship. This celebration of the Portella Massacre, this talking, in its aftermath, of an impending Italian fascist restoration, had a profound and dramatic ring of truth. To explain why, we need to come back to the CMC member who, in 1960, was a key figure, as we already know, of the masonic pact against JFK: Pièche. In fact, the eminent historians Casarrubea and Cereghino, making a clear reference to documents they had consulted, so declare: [298]

In the spring of '47 the project for the coup which had been maturing for a year, came to fruition. Portella della Ginestra was the spark that should have set off the anti-democratic reaction. […] All SIM officials worked on the same wavelength with the Allies, whose commander controlled a secret information office headed by General Marras […]. General Pièche was its hidden inspiration. The office possessed a list of all the leaders of the PCI [Italian Communist Party] and PSI [Italian Socialist Party], who would be arrested "in case of conflict between reds and Allies."

---

[298] ITALIAN DOCUMENT: ACS, Sis, b. 41, *Ministero della Guerra, Ufficio Informazioni Militari*, 8 luglio 1947, segreto

And again: [299]

In the spring of '47, there was talk of a military dictatorship commanded by the Carabinieri [military police] and the top army hierarchy. [...] The ones controlling everything were the Generals [Rodolfo] Corselli and Pièche.

The implications are – to say the least – immense. It means, if we recap what emerged, the existence of a trust at the end of the 1940s between two future CMC members, Spadafora e Pièche, thanks to which a series of anti-Marxist extreme acts were planned and made. This led to that Portella Massacre which was intended to provoke a violent reaction by socialist-communists. This reaction was to be critically used as a pretext for two objectives: one minimal and one maximal, and very close to each other. The minimal one was a ban on the PCI and PSI. The maximal one was precisely the return of fascism to Italy. A feasible goal. The ban, if successful, could have effectively made illegal the two parties busy at that moment, together with the DC, in forging the new Italian Constitution. And by fanning the flames, from this ban there could have been enough chaos to actually block the launch of the Constitution itself. That is, this could have blocked the creation of a document that put a solemn seal on the end of the dictatorship and the rise of a democratic republic. At that point, the return to a fascist nation would have been only a step away.

But fortunately, this audacious plan failed because, on the one hand, showing a great sense of responsibility, both the socialists and the communists managed to control their anger. On the other hand, the plan failed because De Gasperi, after clearly understanding all of the above, had also seen that if the risk was that of being overtaken by much worse events, he then needed to stop his delay in obeying Truman's diktat. And in fact, a month after Portella, he

---

[299] ITALIAN DOCUMENT: ACS, Sis, b. 45, f. LP113/*Unione patriottica anticomunista. Upa*, 1 giugno 1947, segreto

finally formed a government without any more socialists or communists. A decision that led us back to that Bonner's Memorandum of 1948. The Memorandum in which two other future CMC members – Azzaretto and Sagna – conspired so that De Gasperi would be replaced by Gronchi as the DC leader. The same Gronchi who, in 1960, was complicit in the attempted coup by that same Tambroni at the head of a government which was complicit in the masonic pact against JFK. The same Tambroni whose son-in-law Micucci Cecchi was also a CMC member. In other words, Gronchi, with that support to the coup, had proved to be a man without any qualms about carrying out the plan which De Gasperi had refused: a far-right dictatorship.

But there is more. Just close to the Portella massacre, in fact, a series of secret meetings took place in Turin, one of the major cities in northern Italy. The meetings were between Giuliano and the monarchists Alliata di Montereale, Alfredo Covelli and Tommaso Leone Marchesano, all three names later identified by extremely trustworthy sources as instigators of the Sicilian butchery on May 1, 1947. [300] The man running these dealings in Turin was a powerful Freemason, Giuseppe Cambareri, one of the founders of the neo-fascist group *Armata italiana della libertà*. [301] The point is that AIL was captained by Ugo Corrado Musco, yet another CMC member. Not only that but Musco was also named by an Italian source of the OSS hidden under the code-name JK23. This source revealed that Musco was the right-hand man of a general faithful to Mussolini, Roberto Bencivenga who, apart from his powerful contacts with the Freemasons, was at the head of neo-fascist movements. [302] This connection is even stronger in view of the fact that

---

[300] Casarrubea, *Storia segreta della Sicilia*; Casarrubea, *Lupara nera*

[301] Casarrubea, Cereghino, *La scomparsa di Salvatore Giuliano*

[302] ITALIAN DOCUMENT: Acs, fondo Sis, b. 43, f. *Attività monarchica/L25*, Milano, settembre 1946, Oggetto: *Movimento monarchico e neofascista dopo la promulgazione della repubblica*. Cited in: Casarrubea, *Storia segreta della Sicilia*

in 1951, right in the middle of the trial for Portella, Gaspare Pisciotta, who was Giuliano's right-hand man, not only cited as instigators of this massacre the previously mentioned Alliata, Covelli e Marchesano, but also added to them the name of Scelba. And as we know, it was Scelba who put the CMC member Pièche in charge of the *Servizio Antincendi* which disguised a Gladio anti-communism organization. It just so happened that, in the course of his activities at the *Antincendi*, Pièche had protected the aforementioned AIL, as I already explained at the very beginning of this book. [303] And it just so happened that AIL turns up in a letter by Gigliotti. It is a letter dated September 26, 1947, and it is from Gigliotti to the American Under-Secretary of State Norman Armour. Gigliotti speaks of this dangerous terrorist group in very favorable tones, even specifying clearly that AIL was created thanks to the help of the United States. Help which Gigliotti pleads with Armour not to cease giving. These are his words: [304]

All liberal and sincerely democratic [*sic!*] anti-communist Italians groups feel, regarding our government, terribly discouraged and disappointed. They feel we have forgotten about them after we set them up, especially since we helped them create the Italian Freedom Army. And we cannot allow this to happen, because if there should be another war - and God willing, there won't be another one – then we will end up with the same reputation in Italy that we now have in Yugoslavia, that of allowing [the anti-communist Dragoljub] Mihailovic to be hung by Tito.

But there is another equally interesting meeting in Turin we need to talk about. It was in June 1945, and it established the allocation of what today would be some million dollars in order to create in Italy armed anti-communist groups. These groups would be led by Lieutenant Colonel Ernesto Boncinelli, [305] who was not only a very close

---

[303] De Lutiis, *Storia dei servizi segreti in Italia*; Cipriani, *Sovranità limitata*; Murgia, *Ritorneremo!*
[304] Faenza, Fini, *Gli americani in Italia*
[305] Giannuli, *Il Noto servizio*

associate of De Lorenzo, [306] but also one of AIL's coordinators. [307] Really astonishing news. But there is even more, and it is that one of the participants of this meeting in 1945 was actually Valletta. In addition, the renowned essayist and politician Luigi Cipriani, affirmed in one of his studies: [308] "In 1947, Giuliano was still receiving help from the OSS, then CIA, through Gigliotti, on the orders of the boss William Donovan." Moreover, on July 7, 1947 Frank Gigliotti revealed to Saragat, an important right-wing Italian politician, that he had recently met with Giuliano, and that he approved of "the use of illegal means and violence used by Giuliano against the communists." [309]

But, again, this is not all. As it is well explained by Casarrubea and Cereghino, from the first few months of 1946 there was a convergence of views between Italian monarchist and neo-fascist groups and US Intelligence. They were afraid that the result of the referendum on which Italian citizens were preparing to vote would transform the country from a monarchy into a republic. This change was seen as a prelude to a socialist-communist victory in the national elections. For this reason, gaining strength from the pact already sealed with Borghese, the Americans made an agreement with neo-fascist political leaders and members of the armed forces: Augusto Turati, Carlo Scorza, Giovanni Messe, Franco Navarra Viggiani, Pino Romualdi, Nino Buttazzoni. [310] Yes, the very same Buttazzoni ally of Israel.

As a further demonstration that at the root of this alliance there was the pre-existent axis between Angleton and Borghese, this latter in March 1946 was asked by the US Intelligence to organize a paramilitary counter-offensive in case of a socialist-communist victory in the Italian elections. The logistic bulwark of this counter-

---

[306] Andrea Vento, *In silenzio gioite e soffrite*
[307] Giannuli, *Il Noto servizio*
[308] Cipriani, *Appunti sull'anticomunismo dal dopoguerra ad oggi*
[309] Faenza, Fini, *Gli americani in Italia*
[310] Casarrubea, *Lupara nera*

offensive was exactly the biggest Italian island, Sicily. And actually, the X-2 of Rome directed by Angleton, who had created it all, gave the name Operation Sicily to this plan. [311] And it was no coincidence that a few months before, in September 1945, EVIS was formed, which means *Esercito volontario per l'indipendenza della Sicilia* (Voluntary Army for Sicilian Independence). The idea was that the best counteroffensive against this so feared Marxist election victory, was to make Sicily a nation independent from Italy, in order to use it as a military stronghold to regain the rest of the country. [312] It was also no accident that the focal point of EVIS was Giuliano himself. No accident too that Buttazzoni started working for James Angleton in April 1946, with the pseudonym "Engineer Cattarini". At the same time, Buttazzoni founded ECA – *Esercito clandestino anticomunista* (Clandestine Anti-communist Army) – while Romualdi drew up the manifesto of the neo-fascist *Fronte antibolscevico italiano* (Italian Anti-Boshievik Front), immediately delivering it, via Buttazzoni, to Angleton. [313] This manifesto literally affirmed: "The neo-fascists intend to establish a contact with the American authorities to jointly analyze the situation in the country. The Italian political situation will therefore be placed in the hands of the United States." [314]

But pay attention to this: just like the *Armata Italiana della Libertà*, also the FAI was one of those far-right groups whose creation and protection was due to the fundamental help granted by the CMC member Pièche. [315] And once again in 1946, but in October,

---

[311] Casarrubea, *Lupara nera*; Casarrubea, Cereghino, *Portella della Ginestra: documenti su una strage*

[312] Casarrubea, *Lupara nera*; Casarrubea, Cereghino, *Portella della Ginestra: documenti su una strage*

[313] Casarrubea, *Lupara nera*; Casarrubea, Cereghino, *Portella della Ginestra: documenti su una strage*; Casarrubea, Cereghino, *La scomparsa di Salvatore Giuliano*

[314] Casarrubea, *Lupara nera*; Tranfaglia, *Come nasce la Repubblica*

[315] ITALIAN DOCUMENT: Procura della Repubblica di Brescia, Procedimento Penale Nr. 91/97 R.G.N.R. della c.d. "Strage di Piazza della Loggia". Annotazione a cura dell'Ispettore della Polizia di Stato Michele Cacioppo del Servizio Antiterrorismo della Direzione Centrale

here is a document, this time from MI5, the British Intelligence network. It tells of repeated meetings in Rome between the fascist Turati; Pompeo Agrifoglio, ex manager of the *SIM*; Luigi Ferrari, chief of police; Leone Santoro, member of the political office of the Italian Internal Ministry; Angelo Corso, under-secretary in the second De Gasperi government; and finally, a very special person. Philip J. Corso, who was among Angleton's closest collaborators, so much so that he was his main support in dealing with Borghese. [316] The English document specifies: "Numerous American and Italian officers (like the aforesaid Captain Corso) are very closely linked and active in this group". But Philip J. Corso was also mentioned in a British document the following month, which stated: [317]

Captain Corso has recently had a meeting with [the monarchist] Enzo Selvaggi and informed him that he had received instructions from his government to form an anti-communist political group. Corso added that this change of politics was due to the success of the Republican Party in the United States elections [for Congress].

The British spy was author of other documents which are definitely worth dwelling on. Once again traced by Casarrubea and Cereghino, these are dated January 12, January 18, and February 6, 1946, and they all state that in Giuliano's EVIS a very large number of Israelis were fighting, some of them even shuttling between Sicily and Palestine. The British showed surprise. [318] But in the light of what my book explains, it was only seemed a mystery. It is simply

---

della Polizia di Prevenzione concernente l'esame della documentazione relativa all'organizzazione Gehlen" acquisita al SISMI; see also De Lutiis, *Storia dei servizi segreti in Italia*; Cipriani, *Sovranità limitata*; Murgia, *Ritorneremo!*

[316] Casarrubea, *Lupara nera*; Casarrubea, Cereghino, *Portella della Ginestra: documenti su una strage*

[317] Casarrubea, Cereghino, *Portella della Ginestra: documenti su una strage*

[318] Casarrubea, *Lupara nera*; Casarrubea, Cereghino, *Portella della Ginestra: documenti su una strage*

that, once again, even inside EVIS we have that combination of Israelis, Americans and Italian fascists. A combination so massive inside EVIS as to leave no doubt that it also goes through that massacre at Portella which carries the names of three future members of the CMC: Ugo Corrado Musco, Giuseppe Pièche and Gutierez Spadafora. In other words, it confirms the thread between Portella and the opening of the CMC in 1958. Proof of the link is also in the fact that Alliata, associate of Giuliano, was also a Freemason among the supporters of the pact between Italian and American Freemasons; that pact which had the secret clause to stop JFK. Besides, never forget that that pact was signed under the auspices of Tambroni's government. Tambroni's government that, just like any other Italian government, in order to survive needed a vote of confidence from a parliamentary majority; majority that, in the case of Tambroni, was granted thanks to the essential votes from the "missini" (members of the fascist party MSI) and monarchists. Among those monarchists who voted in favor, there was also the aforementioned Alliata, [319] who was also a P2 member and would have been involved in the Borghese coup as well. But another pro-Tambroni monarchist was Falcone Lucifero, [320] who had already been in tough conflict with De Gasperi when the latter had clearly supported the pro-Republic choice in the aforesaid referendum that abolished the monarchy in Italy. [321] All the more reason, apart from what has already been said, to convince Azzaretto and Sagna to view De Gasperi as a weakling who must be replaced as soon as possible. In other words, people who had shown loyalty and reliability to the US far-right extremist groups found themselves, a decade later, part of a plan to return the dictatorship to Italy and, at the same time, to put Nixon, and not JFK, in the White House. This single thread led to

[319] VIE NUOVE: Mafai, *Il marito della contessa Mafalda*, April 16, 1960
[320] VIE NUOVE: Mafai, *Il marito della contessa Mafalda*, April 16, 1960
[321] Oliva, *Gli ultimi giorni della monarchia*; Altieri, *Umberto II e la crisi della monarchia*; Altieri, *Cronaca del Regno d'Italia*

the onset of P2 which was also involved in the deception to prevent Carter from winning a second presidency. Let's see why and how.

CMC AGAINST JIMMY CARTER

We should start with another member of the CMC, Giorgio Zeppieri. He was a lawyer, a profession in which he distinguished himself for absolutely not exemplary behavior. Such as when, with his colleague Rocco Mangia, he was the defense lawyer for the so-called "monsters of Circeo." [322] This case concerned a group of over-excited Italians of extreme right-wing views who, in 1975, raped and tortured two girls on the outskirts of Rome, which ended with such physical violence that one of the girls was killed, while the second saved herself only because she had the presence of mind to pretend she was dead. But Zeppieri was also someone who, as a trial defense lawyer, was extremely offensive in the court-room to a girl who was similarly a victim of a gang rape. [323] But what leads us to Carter is instead contained, even though it may undoubtedly at first seem strange, in an important detail from the psychiatric evaluation that Zeppieri had asked his staff to make against the notorious artist and communist intellectual Pier Paolo Pasolini. The same Pasolini, as we have seen, who in his last book, *Petrolio*, tried to find the truth about the death of Mattei and also the Strategy of Tension. Giorgio Zeppieri, at that time, was legally representing De Santis, a petrol pump attendant who had pressed charges against Pasolini that were ridiculous. He claimed Pasolini had robbed him on November 18, 1961 with a gun, which was never found, and even claimed the artist had loaded it with a golden bullet. From this, Zeppieri managed to spin a yarn in an

---

[322] L'UNITÀ: Paolo Gambescia, *Alla sbarra i massacratori del Circeo sotto accusa della ragazza scampata*, June 29, 1976
[323] Loredana Dordi, *Processo per stupro*

exhausting series of moves which – as Pasolini himself defines it – was intended to morally destroy the artist. The key point of this moral destruction was this psychiatric evaluation. It was signed by the criminologist Aldo Semerari. [324] That signature was what those few who up to now have dwelt on the facts have always noticed, underlining Semerari's adherence to neo-fascism and to P2, but it was unfortunately nonetheless this detail that distracted them from other more important particulars present in the heading of the report. In fact, the heading refers to another name under whose auspices the psychiatric evaluation was compiled: Roberto Zamboni, qualified as scientific director of *Stampa Internazionale Medica* (International Medical Press). Was Zamboni only this? No. I took care to investigate further and discovered that Zamboni appears also in a document on the Strategy of Tension written by the judge Salvini in 1995. Let's read: [325]

Doctor Zamboni effectively belongs to the masonic environment and this confirms the circularity of the relationship between secret organizations, subversive environments of the extreme right and historic organizations of organized crime such as 'ndrangheta. He is a witness to the level of protection that "political soldier" Franco Freda enjoyed for attempting to escape Italian justice.

A support to Salvini's accusations against Zamboni comes from two former *mafiosi*, Filippo Barreca and Giacomo Lauro, who were many times declared highly credible by the legal authorities. The reason why Salvini cites Freda is this fascist terrorist's escape in 1978 after he was arrested for Piazza Fontana. An escape that was protected by an alliance between corrupt Italian state officials and the *'ndrangheta*, which is the Calabrian mafia. One of the principal members of this alliance was Paolo Romeo. Please, note – it is the

---

[324] Umberto Apice, *Processo a Pasolini. La rapina al Circeo*; AA. VV., *Pasolini: cronaca giudiziaria, persecuzione, morte*; Franco Grattarola, *Pasolini. Una vita violentata*
[325] ITALIAN DOCUMENT: *Sentenza-ordinanza del Tribunale di Milano del 18 marzo 1995 n. 2643/84. Procedimento penale nei confronti di AZZI Nico ed altri*

same Romeo Freemason and Italian spy agent whom I mentioned in another part of this book because he was connected to Borghese's neo-fascist coup in 1970. Romeo had been the go-between for Borghese and the *'ndrangheta*, during that attempted overthrow.

In the heading of Semerari's "psychiatric evaluation" of Pasolini there is, however, also an address and a telephone number. I was able to trace these contact details. At the time, they belonged to Giovanni Quattrucci, book editor, but also an editor of magazines. Now, Quattrucci was also a Freemason, as highlighted by an important Italian Court's ruling. I am referring to the one given in July 1985 by the Fifth Assizes Court of Bologna against Francesco Pazienza and others, including Gelli, for the serious crimes of planting evidence concerning the massacre at the Bologna station on August 2, 1980. [326] The point is this: this Court's ruling rightly highlighted an Italian-American association, Great Italy. The Court identified Great Italy as being financed by Italian Intelligence; and more specifically, by SISMI. Great Italy was headed by Quattrucci. As for the other members of Great Italy, apart from Pazienza himself there was also Alfonso (alias Alphonse) Bove. Bove was a figure who had much to do with the dealings of dubious clarity between the P2 member Calvi and the Vatican, and also with events linked to the kidnapping of a famous politician, Ciro Cirillo, a top member of *Democrazia Cristiana*; facts in which Pazienza was involved too. The point is that Great Italy operated nonetheless to favor the US presidential candidate Ronald Reagan. This was done through a scandal falsely created by Pazienza against Billy Carter, the brother of Jimmy Carter, while this latter was busy trying to win his second term in the White House by beating the Republican. More precisely, according to testimonial evidence given by Giuseppe Magnanini, an Italian High Official, the success of "Operation Billygate" was due to

---

[326] ITALIAN DOCUMENT: V Corte D'Assise di Roma, *Sentenza contro Pazienza Francesco, Musumeci Pietro, Belmonte Giuseppe ed altri*, July 29, 1985

the deal struck, in the shadow of Great Italy, between Francesco Pazienza and Michael Ledeen, Ronald Reagan's trusted advisor. [327]

That Great Italy was the key to the truth about the worst vortexes in murky world politics is clearly exposed by an extremely urgent telephone call made by Pazienza to his secretary, ordering him to immediately destroy any material connected to this association. [328] And all this is certainly even more shocking if one considers the links I have already revealed between the CMC and the attempt to kill Carter through the Chilean Klein and the *Banque pour le Commerce Continental*. But it is even more shocking for yet another reason, and that is the fact that Reagan, in order to absolutely win the election, had moreover resorted to a second dirty trick: a secret agreement with the Iranians. In fact, if it was at the start of 1979 that the aforementioned episode to end Carter's life took place, it was towards the end of the same year, precisely on November 4, that the Iranian government held fifty-five members of US diplomatic personnel hostage in Tehran.

This mass kidnapping was due to fears of a possible act of force by Washington; an act to impose the return to power of the Shah of Persia who, thanks to the revolution, the middle-eastern country had just gotten rid of. If those hostages had been liberated by Carter, it is likely that the Democratic candidate would have been re-elected. That is why shady deals were made in Paris between the Republican candidate's *entourage* and the Iranian authorities; to convince the Iranians to end the hostage situation only *after* the end of the presidential elections. And so it happened.

The point is that it was discovered, thanks to a sensational investigation by the Italian journalist Ennio Remondino, that these Parisian meetings included the head of P2, Licio Gelli. [329] But this

---

[327] ITALIAN DOCUMENT: CPP2, Doc XXIII n. *2-quater, Vol. III, Tomo XIX*
[328] ITALIAN DOCUMENT: CPP2, Doc XXIII n. *2-quater, Vol. III, Tomo XIX*
[329] Sergio Flamigni, *Trame atlantiche*; Z MAGAZINE: David Armstrong e Alex Constantine, *The verdict is treason*, July/August 1990; LA REPUBBLICA: *Ennio Caretto, La*

secret pact with the Iranians set off a chain of damaging events resulting in the Iran-Contra Affair, due to the fact that, in compensation, Iran had demanded from Reagan a secret delivery of weapons. The arms that Reagan gave them had arrived thanks to the collusion of Israel, as revealed by both the Tower Commission and the Report of the Congressional Committees Investigating the Iran-Contra Affair. This Israeli collusion was the fruit of the work of Michael Ledeen, Reagan's close advisor, thanks to whom, as we said before, Billygate was a success. In fact, apart from Reagan, Ledeen was also closely connected to Shimon Peres. The sale of illegal arms to Iran was achieved thanks to this pact between Ledeen and the Israeli leader having a brother in the CMC. Yes, it all fits.

CMC AND THE MORO CASE

But according to more than one witness, it was not left to chance that Ledeen was also among those hired by the Italian authorities in order to manage the crisis generated by the kidnapping of Moro. The kidnapping concluded with the politician's assassination, or rather, it ended with the killing of the only survivor, up to that time, of that aforesaid crucial pact to allow the creation, in Italy, of the center-left whose other protagonists had been JFK and Mattei. The job concerning Moro had been given to Ledeen by Cossiga himself, who was Internal Minister during the kidnapping. This fact was confirmed by the psychiatrist and P2 member Franco Ferracuti in an interview to the Italian weekly magazine *Panorama* of June 11, 1988, and reiterated by the member of parliament Umberto Giovine in the sitting on July 15, 1988 of the Italian Parliamentary Commission of Inquiry into the Strategy of Tension.

'nuova guerra' Iraniana di Bush, May 5, 1991; CONSORTIUM NEWS: Robert Parry, *Jimmy Carter's October Surprise dubts*, May 12, 2011

But concerning the kidnapping, we also see the return, once again not by chance, of Roberto Zamboni, the individual linked to that Quattrucci head of Great Italy. Zamboni returns because he was mentioned by the aforesaid former mafioso Lauro. He did this in Court on January 22, 2010 during the trial for the *Piazza della Loggia* massacre, the bloody neo-fascist carnage of 1973 in the Italian city of Brescia. [330] Lauro said that Zamboni, during Moro's kidnapping, was in constant and continuous contact with one of the most powerful P2 members. Who? It was precisely Cosentino, whom we already met through his strong support for Tambroni's attempted coup in 1960. Lauro clarified that the constant contact between Zamboni and Cosentino was due to Cosentino's role as one of the supervisors utilized by P2 to assure a tragic end to that kidnapping, blocking whatever possibility that anyone could liberate Moro. [331] Meanwhile the Red Brigades, author of the kidnapping, were infiltrated by Sogno. An infiltration that, let's not forget, was connected to Sogno's subversive intent supported by the so-called Democratic Resistance Committee the CMC member Bonfantini was part of. It was the same Moro against whom Rocca and Harvey hatched a plan requiring the intervention of the CMC member Crocco. Finally, the same Moro who, as I said before, Cosentino fought against in his 1960 meeting with the USA diplomat Mudd. The meeting where Cosentino, as we know, had described Moro as weak because of his lack of support for the subversive intentions of Tambroni, father-in-law of a member of the CMC. Tambroni's subversive intentions that were fully supported by Cosentino as well.

In other words, we are once again before facts that confirm as totally true the picture of the CMC given by Bellini to the

---

[330] ITALIAN DOCUMENT: Tribunale di Brescia, Corte d'Assise, Procedimento penale n. 003/08 a carico di Carlo Maria Maggi + Altri. Udienza del 22.01.2010
[331] ITALIAN DOCUMENT: Tribunale di Brescia, Corte d'Assise, Procedimento penale n. 003/08 a carico di Carlo Maria Maggi + Altri. Udienza del 22.01.2010

magistrate Calia: "the terminal in Italy of the group who attend to all the dirty work in world politics." Whether the target was JFK, Mattei, Moro, or Carter, or anyone else, it was all the same.

And in fact, during that same testimony during the trial in 2010, Giacomo Lauro, after recounting he had managed to learn Cosentino's most hidden secrets because of a special and privileged relationship with him, pronounced this clear phrase: [332]

They could have returned Moro alive and well, but they didn't want him alive. They didn't want him alive.

We can certainly find confirmation of Lauro's declaration concerning Cosentino's secret role in Moro's death in the fact that *fifty-seven* members of the Italian institutions involved in trying to solve Moro's kidnapping belonged to the P2 headed, besides Gelli, by Cosentino. But we can also find confirmation of the role of *'ndrangheta* in Moro's kidnapping. In fact, let us go back to that document citing Leroy and Merlino, both close associates of the CMC member Pièche, as involved in the Piazza Fontana massacre. That document, we know this too, cites, for the very same reason, also the fascist Delle Chaie. The crux of the matter is that Delle Chiaie, at one point in his life, joined the Condor Network in Chile. This latter was a circle of mutual collaboration and protection among neo-fascist Latin American dictatorships born under the auspices of the CIA. An echo of this can be found in the so-called Archives of Horror of another Latin American nation belonging to the Condor Network, Paraguay. It is a collection of thousands of papers conserved by Alfredo Stroessner, dictator of Paraguay from 1954 until his fall in 1989. This fall generated such a high quantity of chaos as to cause these very incriminating archives to remain

---

[332] ITALIAN DOCUMENT: Tribunale di Brescia, Corte d'Assise, Procedimento penale n. 003/08 a carico di Carlo Maria Maggi + Altri. Udienza del 22.01.2010

unguarded. A situation thanks to which they were found in 1992, fortunately, by Martin Almada, a writer, poet and, above all, activist for human rights. Today, it is Almada who gives interviews about that discovery. In one of them, he is asked: [333]

In the archives they say you even found some documents that would prove the involvement of Italian neo-fascists, including Stefano delle Chiaie, Vincenzo Vinciguerra and Pierluigi Concutelli, in the massacre [in Roma in 1975] of the secretary of the Chilean Christian Democrats Leigthon and their collaboration with the regimes of Pinochet and Stroessner. Is it really true?

Almada replies:

I confirm it. There are documents in which Italian neo-fascists write to Pinochet and Stroessner, making themselves available to fight the Marxist danger. In a letter to Stroessner, Delle Chiaie says he is "an exile because in Italy there is a communist regime." We also found papers that prove that some of the assassins of Aldo Moro were in possession of false Paraguayan papers. We are investigating this to understand if the Moro case had anything to do with Operation Condor.

To picture better what Almada says, we should ideally go to March 16, 1978, the day Moro was kidnapped. Ninety-one bullets were fired in the attack, mostly coming from two people, each responsible respectively for forty-nine and twenty-two shots. The ballistics report established that the shooter of almost fifty cartridges, despite the obvious chaos of a kidnapping of that magnitude, did not miss a single target – a record. This suggests an expert shooter, capable, experienced and far too skillful for it to be an attempt by the Red Brigade alone. One of the top candidates for this role was Giustino De Vuono. Apart from being an ex-soldier in the Foreign Legion – a fact we shall return to later – De Vuono was a member of the 'ndrangheta. [334] His mug shots were actually among those the police issued on the very day

[333] LETTERA 22: Manfredo Pavoni Gay, Almada: Il Condor non è morto, March 29, 2005
[334] Di Giovacchino, Il libro nero della Prima Repubblica

of the kidnapping. But then, suddenly, SISMI, the Intelligence organization full, here we are again, of P2 members, said they were certain – who knows how? – that on that date De Vuono was not in Rome. Now, though, it just so happens that the name in the Archives of Horror discovered by Almada was that of De Vuono. In the archives, there is a briefing of July 4, 1981 addressed to Pastor Coronel, a violator of human rights and close collaborator of Stroessner. This is the start: [335]

I have the honor of addressing your Authority in order to present to you the following information. It concerns exchanges made by Brigadier General Don BENITO GUANES SERRANO, about a person of Italian nationality presumably a member of the ITALIAN RED BRIGADE, the terrorist group, and suspected as one of the assassins of ALDO MORO and to whom the 1st Official LUIS FERNANDEZ, under service of the Dept. of Identifications supplied the Paraguayan Identity Document as citizen of Paraguay:

1. – The subject mentioned of Italian nationality entered our country through Puerto Presidente Stroessner, in the month of June 1977, under the false name of ANTONIO CHIODO, accompanied by a Brazilian citizen named ANECIO DANIEL, in the latter's car, coming from Brazil.

2. – June 22, 1977, the above-mentioned subjects left once again the country from the same place and in the same vehicle, but this time the Italian used his real identity, JUSTINO D'VUONO.

3. – In the month of August 1979, he returned to Paraguay, through Puerto Presidente Stroessner, this time alone, having obtained an Identity Card of Paraguay and a Certificate of Good Conduct as a citizen of Paraguay using the name ANTONIO AGUERO. These documents were organized and forged by 1st Official LUIS FERNANDEZ and a sergeant with the surname MAGGI, in the service of the National Department of Narco-trafficking and Dangerous Drugs. Afterwards Antonio Aguero or Justino D'Vuono left the country.

Notwithstanding the inevitable – but fortunately light – distortion of the foreign name, which is a typically Latin American flaw, it is abundantly clear that the person is the same. But a precise trace of the presence of members of the Calabrian mafia during Moro's

---

[335] PEACE REPORTER, Alessandro Grandi, *Caso Moro: una pista dal Paraguay*, May 13, 2009

kidnapping is also in an Italian document. It is the transcript of a taped telephone conversation between Sereno Freato, Aldo Moro's secretary, and Benito Cazora, a Christian Democrat politician who, with the aim of liberating Moro, managed to establish direct contact with the bosses of Calabrian organized crime. Here it is: [336]

Cazora – I need the photos of March 16th.
Freato – The ones of that place…
Cazora – Yes, because they … (tape here is partially cancelled) it seems that one [of them] is right there. They told me from down there.
Freato – It's that they aren't there. Ah, the photos of them, those nine?
Cazora – No, no. They called me from Calabria to warn me that in one of the photos of the place that morning, you can see someone they know.
Freato – This is a problem.
Cazora – That's why I called you yesterday.
Freato – What can we do? We need to think for a moment. Listen. Tell the minister. There'll be a lot [of photos].
Cazora – A copy, you understand, may be in the papers on March 16, or 17.

And the fact that in the phone call they were talking about a photo showing 'ndrangheta members, is confirmed today by Marco Cazora, Benito's son. He said this in interview with a specialist on the Moro Affair, Manlio Castronuovo. The interview specifies how his father had then paid with the end of his political career the intention to bring the 'ndrangheta onto the side of those wanting to release Moro, and to cancel the plans of those who had already agreed to end the life of the hostage. [337]

De Vuono – pay attention – is mentioned also by an eye-witness who recognized him as a visitor to the edifice in Via Gradoli (Gradoli Street) in Rome, a BR hide-out linked to the statesman's kidnapping. Moreover, we should add an article published on January 16, 1979,

---

[336] Di Giovacchino, *Il libro nero della Prima Repubblica*
[337] VUOTO A PERDERE: Manlio Castronuovo, *Intervista a Marco Cazora*, December 25, 2007

by the constantly well-informed journalist Pecorelli, who, describing the past of De Vuono in the Foreign Legion, writes: [338]

And the BR would have killed the president of the DC in the car, in the center of Rome, with all the risks that such an operation would have. But we won't talk about that, because it is a theory of mind games, up in the air. We won't say that the legionary was called "De" and the butcher Maurizio

Having clarified everything needed about De Vuono, it is finally time to go back to Delle Chiaie. In fact, as recounted by witnesses, the latter, before going to Chile, had just been to Calabria. One of these witnesses was Giacomo Lauro. Here it is a significant piece of one of his interrogations: [339]

LAURO: […] **DELLE CHIAIE** had been to [the Calabrian city] Reggio in 1970 as a guest [of Carmine Dominici], *his* guest, and of **Fefè ZERBI**, and of **Fefè ZERBI**. So, you can question Mr. **DOMINICI** about these circumstances.
P.M.: But **DELLE CHIAIE** had contact also …
LAURO: Yes, yes, he had contact …
P.M.: … with members of the 'ndrangheta …
LAURO: He had contact, he had contact with **Paolo DE STEFANO**.
P.M.: And how do you know this?
LAURO: He told me.
P.M.: Dominici?
LAURO: Yes …

This means that Delle Chiaie in Calabria visited *exactly* the same circles connected to Franco Freda's escape; the escape protected by Zamboni. It means the very same Zamboni also accomplice of the CMC member Zeppieri when they both acted against Pasolini. Zamboni who was also an accomplice, during the Moro kidnapping, of the P2 member Cosentino.

---

[338] Sergio Flamigni, *Le Idi di Marzo*; Di Giovacchino, *Il libro nero della Prima Repubblica*
[339] ITALIAN DOCUMENT: Direzione Investigativa Antimafia - Centro Operativo Reggio Calabria, *Informativa Olimpo, PARTE V, ESPANSIONE TERRITORIALE E DEVIANZE, C) Massoneria, pubbliche istituzioni e servizi*, 1994

But Delle Chiaie's presence in Calabria was also written about in one of the last articles of Giovanni Spampinato; it was one of the last because in 1972 the journalist was killed. A killing that many relate exactly to this article's content. [340] Some admission, albeit partial, belated, and with the hint of an indirect message to others, came from Delle Chiaie himself in an interview to a newspaper in October 2012. He there admitted he had had Calabrian contacts. And when specifying them, the neo-fascist cites the same name as Lauro did, saying: [341]

It was Fefè Zerbi and other comrades. Some of them are dead and others live their lives, so it isn't up to me to say who they were. This is not a problem. The one responsible was Felice Zerbi. Once there was also Ciccio Franco, who was close to, actually he was part of, the National Front and Avanguardia [Nazionale]. There were a lot. There was [Giuseppe] Schirinzi. There were lots of people. It's useless saying all the names because it doesn't make sense today.

But in the same interview, when he was asked about his movements in Calabria, Delle Chiaie, strangely losing his famously excellent memory, came out with this faulty, minimizing answer: [342]

I don't remember, maybe in '74, possibly ... don't know. I moved about a lot, so I don't remember. But if I was there it was for some meeting with a comrade who had problems or to solve some internal problem. I didn't do any more. I didn't have the political power to work.

But there is even another element which proves Lauro was right. It emerged in 2015, when the Italian parliamentary commission of inquest to investigate the Moro Affair studied the story of a mysterious bar overlooking the place where Moro was kidnapped. The

---

[340] Luciano Mirone, *Gli insabbiati*
[341] IL DISPACCIO: Alessia Candito, *Stefano Delle Chiaie "la ndrangheta non poteva opporsi ai Moti di Reggio"*, October 15, 2012
[342] IL DISPACCIO: Alessia Candito, *Stefano Delle Chiaie "la ndrangheta non poteva opporsi ai Moti di Reggio"*, October 15, 2012

parliamentary commission discovered that this bar was run at the moment of the kidnapping by a company, Olivetti, founded, as the name implies, by a certain Tullio Olivetti. It was the same Tullio Olivetti who, by the way, also appeared in the lists, drawn up by the Bologna Police, of the people present in the Emilian city in the days immediately preceding the massacre of August 2, 1980. [343] The very same massacre, which for having planted evidence, Francesco Pazienza, member of Great Italy, and Licio Gelli, head of the P2 lodge so indistinguishable from CMC, were found guilty. But on the Board of Directors of Olivetti sat also Maria Cecilia Gronchi, the daughter of the former President of the Italian Republic Gronchi, the great friend of Tambroni... [344]

---

[343] LA REPUBBLICA: Alberto Custodonero, *Caso Moro, i palestinesi avvertirono l'Italia*, December 10, 2015

[344] LA REPUBBLICA: Alberto Custodonero, *Caso Moro, i palestinesi avvertirono l'Italia*, December 10, 2015

CONCLUSION

Well, I have come to the end of my study of the interconnections between CMC and the Kennedy case. I am certain that it has shown, on the one hand, how persistently Centro Mondiale Commerciale was dedicated to getting rid of essential political leaders in the world and of people who CMC considered too inconvenient to leave them alive. On the other hand, I think it has also shown how necessary it is for the Israelis of good will – of which there are many – to demand with a loud voice the emersion of the full truth concerning their country's role in the assassination of JFK. If this is done, it will truly permit the rise of an invincible alliance between people of authentic democratic spirit, and enable the creation of an International Court to prosecute those responsible for the Strategy of Tension in Italy, the assassination of JFK in Dallas, and the wrong-doings that today plague the destiny of Israel, plunging it down into a situation that the Jews exterminated by the gas chambers would certainly be ashamed of. Anyone instead wanting to use my book to shout stupid phrases like "Hitler was right" or "Death to Israelis" or similar, should know that they are committing a crime, they did not understand anything of what I have explained in these pages, and that, more in general, they do not understand life and they are not my friends. My concluding thoughts go to JFK. Thank you for your courage, your generosity, your wisdom. May this, my heartfelt work, also be my ideal embrace for you.

APPENDIX
- DOCUMENTS -

Please, note: watermark added.

10) Avv.Franco Micucci;

11) Dott.Ferenc Nagy;

12) Gr.Uff.Angelo Sagna;

13) Hans Seligman-Schürch;

14) Clay Shaw;

4) di dare facoltà e mandato ai sunnominati Consiglieri di nominare per cooptazione l'altro Consigliere fino al raggiungimento del numero di quindici;

5) di nominare per un triennio il Collegio Sindacale della Società nelle persone dei Signori:

- Dott.Etelberto Vitale- iscritto all'Albo dei Dot-
tori Commercialisti Revisori Ufficiali dei Conti-
Presidente;

- Corrado Bertagnoli, Sindaco effettivo;

- Mariano Recchi, Sindaco effettivo;

- Rag.Luigi Emilio Ravaro-iscritto all'Albo dei Dot-
tori Commercialisti-Revisori Ufficiali dei Conti-
Sindaco supplente.

- Dott.Franco Agnesi-Sindaco supplente.

Dei sunnominati Consiglieri di Amministrazione, i
Signori Avv.Carlo d'Amelio, Dott.Enrico Mantello,
On.le Mario Ceravolo, Dott.Ferenc Nagy e Hans Seligman-Schürch, essendo presenti dichiarano di accettare la carica loro conferita e che nei propri confronti non sussiste alcuna delle cause di ineleggi-

il 17.3.1897 e domiciliato a Roma;

4) Avv. Virgilio Gaito, nato a Napoli il 1.5.1930 e domiciliato a Roma;

5) Avv. Franco Musco, nato a Roma il 3.10.1929 ed ivi domiciliato.

L'Assemblea infine nomina una Commissione composta dai Sigg.:

1) Dr. Monir Spahi;

2) Dr. Nicolas Fisher;

3) Geom. Pasquale Palange;

con l'incarico di compilare una relazione generale sulle cause che hanno determinato il ritardato sviluppo dell'attività sociale.

Non avendo nessuno chiesto la parola ed essendo esauriti gli argomenti posti all'Ordine del Giorno, alle ore quattordici e trenta il Presidente dichiara sciolta l'assemblea.

Letto, approvato e sottoscritto.

IL PRESIDENTE
f.to Franco Mancuso

IL SEGRETARIO
f.to Pasquale Palange

per copia conforme il Presidente Franco Mancuso

zione e l'intero Collegio Sindacale si sono resi

dimissionari e pertanto anche in relazione al deli-

berato aumento del capitale sociale con la probabile

formazione di nuovi gruppi azionari, si rende op-

portuna la nomina ex novo degli organi amministra-

tivi e di controllo.

L'Assemblea, preso atto delle dichiarazioni del Pre-

sidente, alla unanimità delibera:

1) di fissare a norma dell'Articolo 13 dello Statu-

to Sociale, in 15 (quindici) il numero dei componen-

ti il Consiglio di Amministrazione;

2) di stabilire la durata del nominando Consiglio

di Amministrazione in un triennio dalla data di og-

gi;

3) di nominare Consiglieri di Amministrazione, per

il suddetto periodo, i Signori:

1) On.le Gaetano Alberti;

2) Cav.del Lav.Giuseppe Azzaretto;

3) Dott.Sergio Casaltoli;

4) On.le Mario Ceravolo;

5) Avv.Carlo d'Amelio,

6) Dott.Manlio Germozzi;

7) Dott.Oreste Giannetti;

8) P.pe Dott.Gutierez di Spadafora;

9) Dott.Enrico Mantello;

6) Nomina del Comitato Direttivo;

7) Convocazione dell'Assemblea dei Soci per l'amplia
mento del numero dei Consiglieri e nomine relative;

8) Varie ed eventuali.

Sul primo numero dell'O.d.G. il Presidente ricorda
che con deliberazione assembleare del 22 aprile 1958
è stato dato mandato al Consiglio di Amministrazione di procedere alla nomina di un terzo Consigliere
di Amministrazione.

Il Dott. Mario Mantello propone che sia chiamato a
ricoprire tale carica il Principe Dott. Guglielmo di
Spadafora.

Il Consiglio approva la proposta del Cons. Mantello.

Il Presidente, essendo a conoscenza che il Dott. Spa
dafora trovasi nei locali adiacenti a quelli ove si
svolge il Consiglio, invita il medesimo ad interve-
nire alla riunione. Avuta la presenza del Principe
di Spadafora il Presidente gli rivolge a nome della
Società un caldo saluto ed un augurio di una profi-
cua collaborazione.

Il Principe Spadafora ringrazia il Presidente e la
Società per la particolare considerazione dimostra-
ta e dichiara di accettare l'incarico.

Passando al n.2 dell'O.d.G. prende la parola il Con-sei mesi alla nomina per coptazione degli altri Con   . 3.

siglieri i cui posti restano vacanti.

L'Assemblea approva all'unanimità, per cui il Consi-

glio di Amministrazione resta così costituito:

1) On.Corrado Bonfantini-Deputato al Parlamento-Roma

2) On.Mario Ceravolo-Deputato al Parlamento-Roma

3) Avv.Carlo d'Amelio - Roma

4) Duca Gutierez di Spadafora - Palermo

5) Dr. Ernet Feisst - Ministro Svizzero - Berna

6) Prof. Max Hagemann - Editore - Basilea

7) Dr. Enrico Mantello - Basilea

8) Dr.Ferenc Nagy - Ex Primo Ministro d'Ungheria

9) Prof.Edgard Salin-Professore Università-Basilea

10.) Hans Seligman-Schurch-Banca Seligman Schurch -

       Basilea

11) Clay Shaw - Cons.Deleg.Fiera Internazionale Per-

       manente di New Orleans.

I Consiglieri presenti dichiarano di accettare, rin-

graziando.

Sugli argomenti vari nessuno chiede la parola e,per-

tanto, l'Assemblea è sciolta alle ore 13 e 30 (tre-

dici e trenta).

     IL SEGRETARIO   IL PRESIDENTE

  F.to E. Mantello   F.to Avv.Carlo d'Amelio

          - - - - - - - -

169

Franco Ostini,Geom.Sig.Massimo Londei,avv.Giorgio
Tappieri,oltre che di sè medesimo,quale Presidente
(non presente soltanto il Consigliere avv.Roberto
Ascarelli) nonchè la presenza del Collegio Sindacale
nelle persone dei sigg. : Dott.Vitale Etelberto,Pre-
sidente; dott.Iammuzzi Michele –Sindaco effettivo;
Ragioniere Maurizi Erменно,Sindaco effettivo;
dichiara l'assemblea legalmente costituita per deli-
berare validamente sugli argomenti posti all'ordine
del giorno.
Prende la parola il Presidente dell'assemblea,il quale sul punto "1" dell'ordine del giorno,relazione
sull'andamento degli affari sociali e in particolare
dà notizia che egli si è avvalso della cooperazione
e collaborazione del sig.avv.Franco Musco per una
serie di operazioni bancarie e finanziarie e di as-
sunzione di obbligazioni,cambiarie poste in essere
a firma congiunta e chiede che tali operazioni venga-
no ratificate dall'assemblea.
L'assemblea,all'unanimità ratifica ed approva ogni
operazione svolta nel modo suddetto dal Presidente
e dall'avv.Franco Musco esonerando quest'ultimo da
ogni e qualsiasi responsabilità al riguardo.
Sul punto due il Presidente fa presente che si rende
necessario per ovvi motivi,modificare l'art.17 (di-

170

VERBALE DEL CONSIGLIO D'AMMINISTRAZIONE

Il giorno 13 novembre 1964, alle ore 19, presso la sede sociale in Roma - viale della Tecnica - a seguito di avviso di convocazione si è riunito il Consiglio di Amministrazione della società-

ORDINE DEL GIORNO:

1) Elezione delle cariche sociali-

2) Varie ed eventuali-

Il Consiglio delibera di nominare Vice Presidente della Società con tutti i poteri del Presidente in caso di assenza o impedimento di questo, l'avv. Franco Musco con l'intesa di proporre la modifica relativa dello Statuto alla prossima assemblea straordinaria da convocarsi entro breve termine-

Il Consiglio ratifica tutti gli atti fin qui compiuti dall'avv. Franco Musco a favore della Società ringraziandolo della sua opera -

Il Consiglio di Amministrazione delibera all'unanimità di nominare presidente del Consiglio di Amministrazione della Società l'On.le Avv. Alfredo Crocco con tutti i poteri di legge e dello Statuto Sociale -

L'On.le Avv. Alfredo Crocco e l'Avv. Franco Musco dichiarano di accettare la carica ad essi conferita. Dichiarano altresì che nei propri confronti

171

a favore della società.-

Il presidente del Consiglio di Amministrazione Sig.Giorgio

Mantello fa presente che a norma dell'art.2386 C.C. il

consiglio è chiamato a nominare due consiglieri per opta-

zione.- Ad unanimità dei consiglieri presenti vengono nomi-

nati , con l'approvazione dei sindaci presenti, consiglieri

di amministrazione con tutti i poteri di legge e dello

Statuto sociale i Signori :

1)- Gershon Perez, nato il 5 gennaio 1926 a Vishniv (Polonia)

e domiciliato a Tel Aviv Zamenhof 31 Israele, cittadino

israeliano ;

2)- Avv.Valentino Benedetti nato a Napoli il 2 giugno 1941

e domiciliato in Roma Via Alfredo Serranti n.13, cittadino

italiano.-

I nuovi eletti vengono introdotti nella sala del Consiglio

ed il presidente dà loro comunicazione dell'avvenuta nomina.

I Signori Perez e Avv.Benedetti ringraziano e dichiarano di

accettare la carica ad essi conferita, dichiarando altresì

che nei propri confronti non sussistono cause di ineleggi-

bilità o di decadenza di cui all'art.2382 del Codice Civile.

Il Consiglio nomina vice presidente del Consiglio di Ammi-

nistrazione con tutti i poteri di legge e dello Statuto so-

ciale il Dott.Alberto Forte, che,presente, dichiara di

accettare la carica ad esso conferita.-

    Non avendo nessuno chiesto la parola la seduta è tolta

172

Roma, Via Vittorio Veneto 54/B - al quale vengono conferiti

i seguenti poteri:

a) sovraintendenza agli uffici della Società;

b) firma individuale che gli permetta di procedere alle opera

zioni necessarie sul conto della Società presso la Banca Na

zionale del Lavoro.

Il Consiglio prega il Presidente Sig. Giorgio Mantello di effet

tuare le pratiche necessarie affinché il Sig. Arié Ben-Tovim

abbia la residenza stabile in Italia per poter proficuamente

svolgere l'attività a cui è stato preposto.

Essendo esauriti gli argomenti posti all'ordine del giorno e

non avendo nessuno chiesto la parola, alle ore dieci e trenta

la seduta è tolta.

Letto, approvato e sottoscritto.

Il Segretario

F.to Dott. Vitale   F.to Il Presidente

Sociali.

L'Assemblea fissa in sei il numero dei comparenti
ed all'unanimità elegge i seguenti Consiglieri:

1) dott. DI PILATO DOMENICO -

2) Gen.PIECHE GIUSEPPE -

3) Comm.PUGGIONI ANNETTO -

4) Comm.Brembilla Gino -

5) Dott.Nikolaus FISCHER -

6) On.Odo Spadazzi -

A Presidente del Consiglio di Amministrazione viene confermato il Comm.Odo Spadazzi, che accetta.

Il nuovo Collegio Sindacale viene così eletto:

1) Dott.Iannuzzi Michele - Revisore Ufficiale dei
Conti - Presidente

2) Dott.Dante De Benedetti - Sindaco effettivo -

3) Avv.D'Errico Giovanni - Sindaco Effettivo -

A sindaci supplenti vengono eletti:

1) Dott.Domenico Ferretti - revisore Ufficiale dei
Conti

2) Palange Antonio - Sindaco supplente -

Per i punti seguenti all'ordine del giorno, si dà
mandato al Consiglio di Amministrazione.

Essendo esaurita la parte ordinaria, la presente
assemblea si chiude, per procedere con la parte
straordinaria con verbale notarile.

174

Made in the USA
Middletown, DE
10 February 2019